2194

D0689742

VICTORIAN CHRISTMAS

VICTORIAN CHRISTMAS

Over 50 ideas for enjoying a Traditional Christmas

VALERIE JANITCH

Anaya Publishers Ltd
LONDON

First published in 1993 by Anaya
Publishers Ltd, 44–50 Osnaburgh Street,
London NW1 3ND

British Library Cataloguing in
Publication Data.
Janitch, Valerie
Victorian Christmas
I Title
745.594
ISBN 1–85470–069–3

Text Editor: Eve Harlow
Photography and styling: Di Lewis
Food photography: Patrick McLeavey
Home economist: Annie Nichols
Designer: Sheila Volpe
Artwork: Coral Mula, Michael Volpe
Picture research: Annette Balfour Lynn
Typeset in Cochin by Art Photoset Ltd,
Beaconsfield, UK
Colour origination by Scantrans Pte Ltd,
Singapore
Printed and bound in Malaysia by
Times Offset (M) Sdn Bhd

CONTENTS

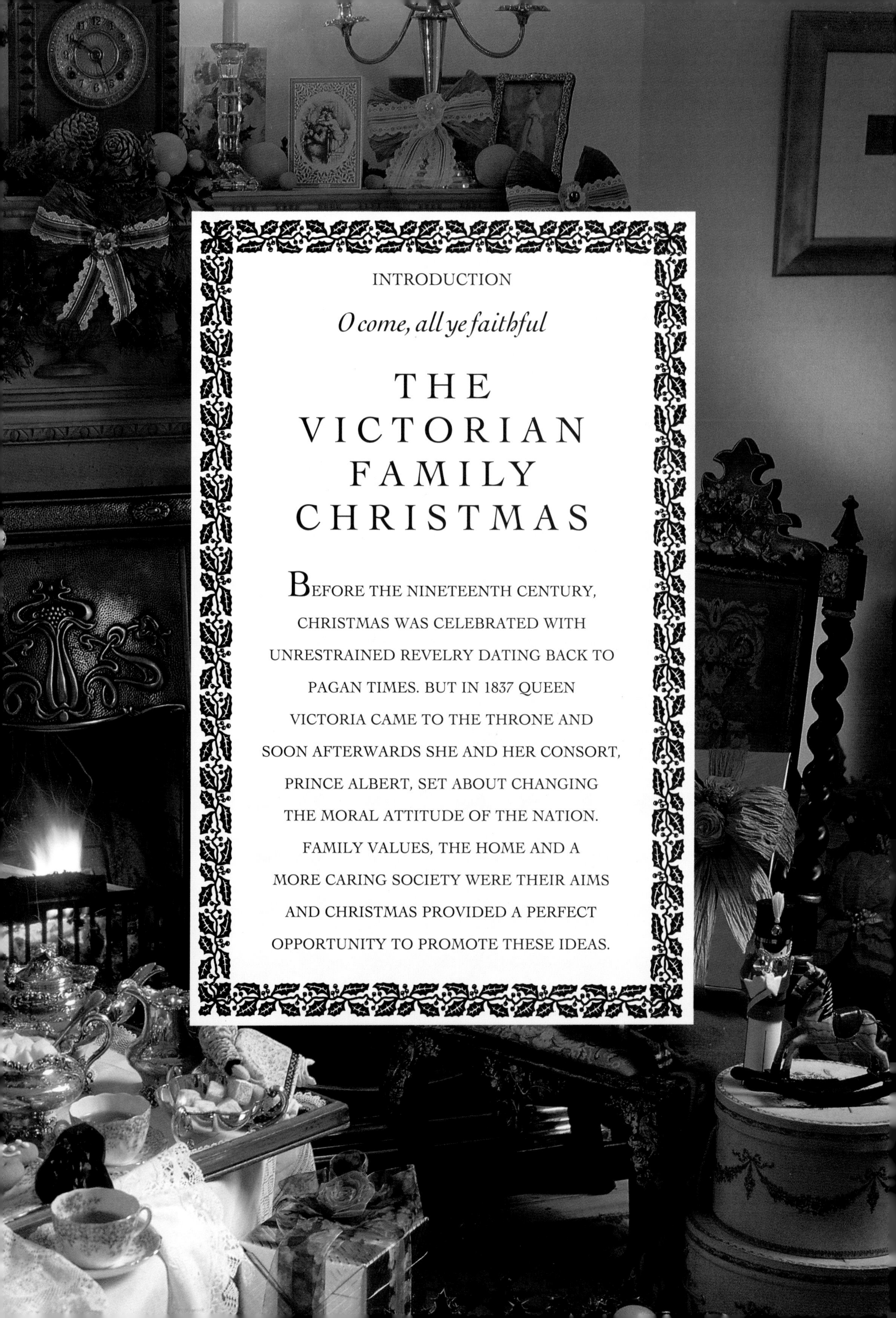

INTRODUCTION

O come, all ye faithful

THE VICTORIAN FAMILY CHRISTMAS

BEFORE THE NINETEENTH CENTURY,
CHRISTMAS WAS CELEBRATED WITH
UNRESTRAINED REVELRY DATING BACK TO
PAGAN TIMES. BUT IN 1837 QUEEN
VICTORIA CAME TO THE THRONE AND
SOON AFTERWARDS SHE AND HER CONSORT,
PRINCE ALBERT, SET ABOUT CHANGING
THE MORAL ATTITUDE OF THE NATION.
FAMILY VALUES, THE HOME AND A
MORE CARING SOCIETY WERE THEIR AIMS
AND CHRISTMAS PROVIDED A PERFECT
OPPORTUNITY TO PROMOTE THESE IDEAS.

Nostalgia is a wonderful thing, enabling us to imagine how things were before we were born. Or, when recalling our own memories, it permits us to forget the things we'd rather *not* remember! Woodland walks hand-in-hand; idyllic picnics; exotic holidays; weddings and anniversaries… in retrospect they were so utterly perfect. Wasps and hungry insects, rain and travel problems, wet feet and head colds all fade into oblivion. That's the special magic of nostalgia; it makes the past so much more comfortable.

Along with long hot summers, Christmas must surely be the best excuse to indulge in nostalgia. We dream about an old-fashioned 'traditional Christmas'. The sparkling frost crunching underfoot on the way to Midnight Mass. The candle-lit tree decorated with tinsel and baubles. The house adorned with holly, ivy, mistletoe – and carol singers at the door. Gifts wrapped in shiny paper tied with gigantic ribbon bows. Cards on the mantelpiece above a glowing log fire. The breathless excitement of a child opening the stocking that Santa filled when he came down the chimney. These are the nostalgic scenes that evoke our idea of a traditional nineteenth-century Christmas.

Life for the English Victorian middle-class was made easy by servants who washed and ironed, cooked and scrubbed and swept, cleaned the grates, lit the lamps and looked after the children. Today, the servants are replaced by washing machines, easy-care fabrics, microwave ovens, vacuum cleaners, central heating, and all the other labour-saving wonders of modern technology and the microchip.

As the much-loved novels of Charles Dickens demonstrate, while many English families of the mid-nineteenth century lived in leisured comfort, seeking agreeable pastimes to fill their time, the poorer people lived in appalling conditions. Thousands of them left the countryside for the cities and towns to find work in the factories of the Industrial Revolution. At the same time, a new middle-class society emerged – those who profited from this economic growth. As the better-off became aware of the starvation, illness and drunkenness that resulted from the poverty, consciences were pricked. The bleak midwinter made Christmas a special time for goodwill and generosity. In Dickens' *A Christmas Carol*, even the miserly Scrooge was forced to recognize the joy of Christmas.

There is much to be sad about in the world today, just as there was in the Victorian era. But this is a book of nostalgia, remembering the good times of the nineteenth century as Queen Victoria *wanted* it to be. She tried to encourage her subjects with her own example of a happy family gathered around a fir tree hung with pretty decorations: a day when people everywhere stop to greet one another in peace and harmony, exchanging cards and presents to

ABOVE: Children were a favourite subject for Victorian Christmas cards. The Christmas stocking derives from a legendary story about St Nicholas, patron saint of children.

BELOW: 'I'm crying because I've eaten too much and I've no room for the pudding.' (Cartoon from The London Illustrated News.)

demonstrate friendship and love.

This sense of family was vividly reflected by all those who had crossed the Atlantic to find a better life in America. Far from home, Christmas was a very sentimental time for them, evoking their own specially poignant nostalgia. It was a time to recall the countries of their birth in their own particular way, with national customs remembered from childhood. Perhaps this is why celebrating a 'traditional Christmas' has as much meaning in the United States as in Queen Victoria's own country.

In *Victorian Christmas*, decorations, table settings, cards and gifts are inspired by the best of Victorian design, yet have a fresh contemporary approach. Food and drink, games and customs are recalled as we recreate the festive season in modern mood. Decorative crafts of the 1800s are revived with all the advantages of 1990s fabrics and materials that make every kind of craftwork easy and enjoyable, as well as achieving the speedy results that our busier lifestyle demands.

So you can forget the problems, and re-live all the pleasures of Victorian Christmas crafts with the benefit of modern equipment. The Victorians would be the first to agree: nostalgia is a wonderful thing!

This wonderfully evocative painting, The Christmas Tree *by Albert Chevallier Tayler, shows how, as Queen Victoria's reign neared its end, the Victorian family Christmas was already established as a much-loved tradition.*

By this time it was getting dark, and snowing pretty heavily; and as Scrooge and the Spirit went along the streets, the brightness of the roaring fires in kitchens, parlours, and all sorts of rooms was wonderful. Here, the flickering of the blaze showed preparations for a cosy dinner, with hot plates baking through and through before the fire, and deep red curtains, ready to be drawn to shut out cold and darkness. There, all the children of the house were running out into the snow to meet their married sisters, brothers, cousins, uncles, aunts, and be the first to greet them. Here, again, were shadows on the window-blinds of guests assembling; and there a group of handsome girls, all hooded and fur-booted, and all chattering at once, tripped lightly off to some near neighbour's house; where, woe upon the single man who saw them enter – artful witches: well they knew it – in a glow.

From *A Christmas Carol* by Charles Dickens

CHAPTER ONE

In the bleak mid-winter...

TRADITIONAL DECORATIONS

THE VICTORIAN CELEBRATIONS WERE VERY DIFFERENT FROM THE WILD EXCESSES OF PREVIOUS CENTURIES. BUT DECORATING WITH EVERGREENS, FIRE AND LIGHT WAS ONE TRADITION THAT WAS TOO DEEPLY INGRAINED TO BE ABANDONED. LONG BEFORE CHRISTIANITY, PAGANS ALL OVER EUROPE CELEBRATED THE WINTER SOLSTICE IN THIS WAY, SYMBOLIZING THE COMING OF SPRING AND FERTILITY. ALL KINDS OF STRANGE SUPERSTITIONS ARE ATTACHED TO CHRISTMAS EVERGREENS, HOLLY, IVY AND MISTLETOE, WHILE CANDLES ARE DEEPLY SYMBOLIC.

Decorating the house with greenery and lighted candles at the end of the year was traditional long before Christianity began. For many pagan peoples the winter solstice marked the turn of the year, reminding them that spring would soon be on the way. It was celebrated with festivals of fire and light, making a welcome break in the dark winter months. Evergreens were used for decoration, symbolizing fertility as the days lengthened and the sun grew stronger, bringing a renewal of life and growth and the promise of fresh crops.

As the Roman Empire spread, so did its great festival of Saturnalia, which began on the 17th of December and led up to the 25th, the day that the Romans observed as the Birthday of the Unconquered Sun. Wild behaviour was encouraged: men dressed in animal skins, and master and servant exchanged clothes and identities, as an excuse to indulge in all kinds of outrageous misconduct. Laurel wreaths and branches decorated the houses, and lamps burned continuously.

Immediately after Saturnalia came Kalends – a three-day festival to celebrate the New Year. This less exuberant celebration was presided over by Strenia, the goddess of health, and greenery from her groves was wound into wreaths and exchanged as gifts. These were fixed to the door of the house to ensure the health of everyone who lived there in the forthcoming year.

In Northern Europe, the winter solstice was marked by the festival of Yule. The short, dark days, icy winds and intense cold were made more bearable by blazing fires and glowing lamps. Evergreens decorated the houses, and gifts were made as sacrifices to the great Norse gods, Odin and Thor, and the goddess Frey. Likewise, the druids, priests of the religion of early Celtic Britain, built shrines of greenery to shelter spirits of the woods during the dark winter months, and ensure a survival into spring.

The early Christians were undecided when to celebrate the birthday (or Mass) of Christ, and chose various dates – as far apart as the 1st and 6th of January, the 29th of March and the 29th of September. Towards the end of the fourth century, the Church Fathers felt it necessary to fix a definite date, and the Pope wisely decided on the 25th of December. Realizing that it was almost impossible to eradicate the traditional Roman, Nordic and Celtic festivals, which were psychologically important to the people's lives and so greatly enjoyed at this season of the year, it seemed more sensible to include them into the Christmas celebrations. Which explains why so many of the pagan rituals of Saturnalia, Kalends and Yule – the evergreen life-symbols, the yule logs and candlelight – are still with us today.

An American lover and his lass weave holly wreaths, perpetuating a tradition dating back to the Roman festivals celebrating the winter solstice, and introduced to the United States by Scandinavian settlers.

Holly, ivy and mistletoe are the evergreens that are immediately associated with Christmas. The scarlet-berried holly provides a bright note when there is so little colour available in the hedgerows, which is probably why the early Christian church adopted it – suggesting that the prickly leaves represented Christ's crown of thorns, and the berries drops of His blood. As a symbol of eternal life, it meant good fortune – especially if it had been used to decorate the church. The people of the state of Louisiana in southern USA always kept the berries for luck, and holly hung in the cowshed on Christmas Eve is said to ensure the health of the occupants. For humans, holly was used to treat fevers, dropsy and rheumatism, gout and asthma, while the North American Indians treated measles with holly tea.

The blazing Yule log and energetic revelry of the pagan winter festivities called, of course, for something special in the way of thirst-quenching drinks. In English country villages especially, the traditional Christmas drinks were still an important part of the festivities in Victorian times. These ranged from 'egg-hot' – heated cider mixed with eggs and spices – to 'ale posset', a concoction of ale and hot milk, sweetened and flavoured with sugar and spices, which was always the final drink on Christmas Eve.

Christmas Morning by Thomas Falcon, shows the sentimentality typical of the period. Poor children trudge through the snow bringing bunches of holly, gathered from the woods, to the church porch, in the hope of earning a few precious pennies from devout worshippers.

A donkey burdened with holly plods through deep snow. The romantic white Christmas was as common on Victorian cards as it is now. But in fact snowbound Christmases were as rare in the nineteenth century as they have been in England in the twentieth.

Ivy, when combined with holly, ensured fertility within the house and, when it grew on the walls outside, it kept the occupants safe from witches. Medicinally, the leaves were used to treat ulcers, abscesses and corns; and constant wearing of an ivy wreath was thought to prevent falling hair!

Mistletoe, on the other hand, was banned from churches because of its pagan connections. It was important to both the druids and the Norsemen as protection against fire and earth and water, but it was especially sacred to the druids, who believed mistletoe was doubly powerful when growing on an oak, which they consider the father of the trees. Known as 'Heal-all' for its herbal qualities, the Celtic high priest cut the mistletoe with a golden sickle.

It was also the symbol of everlasting love, and in Victorian England, mistletoe was used as an innocent excuse for a kiss. But in country districts it was essential to keep some in the home as a protection from thunder, lightning, spells and all kinds of other evil.

In the centuries before Prince Albert's successful promotion of the fir tree, the traditional British Christmas decoration was an enormous garland of greenery called a 'kissing bough', which was hung in the centre of the main room. Hoops of willow were woven with holly, ivy, mistletoe and yew, and hung with rosy apples, under a circle of candles. Beneath it the revellers sang carols, danced, acted plays – and, of course, kissed. The candles were lit on Christmas Eve, and then again each evening until Twelfth Night.

The customs and superstitions associated with Christmas greenery are countless. Don't sit under a pine tree on Christmas Eve: you will hear the angels sing – but you'll be dead soon after! Don't bring evergreens into the house before Christmas Eve. And after Christmas, they mustn't be taken down before Twelfth Night. Church decorations could remain until Candlemas – but every leaf that remained behind after that date (February 2nd) meant bad luck.

Don't burn green holly: that's unlucky too. But disposal was largely a matter of geographical location. In some districts, when the Christmas decorations were taken down the holly must be left to wither and die – in others it must be burnt. However, a sprig might be retained to carry its good luck into the New Year. Mistletoe, too, must be burnt after Twelfth Night: otherwise the couples who kissed under it might never marry.

Candles represented purity and cleansing, as well as new life. A Yule candle left in the centre of the table to burn through Christmas Eve would ensure good luck in the coming year. The tallow was also believed to have magic properties, and the Swedish farmer rubbed the wax into the blades of his plough for fertility when he prepared his fields for the spring sowing. The remains of the candle would be re-lit to protect the house during thunder storms.

Christianity changed the meaning of candlelight, using it to represent Christ as the Light of the World. In Germany and Sweden, special Advent candles are lighted to mark the Advent period – the four weeks before Christmas. Swedish homes are visited on 13th December by St Lucia, the Swedish patron Saint of Light, dressed in white and red to represent light and fire, and wearing a crown of candles. While in southern Germany, Frau Berchta, their Goddess of Light, appears on the 6th of January.

During the eight-day Jewish festival of Hannukah in mid-December, candles are lighted each day, commemorating the rededication of the temple after it had been cleansed of pagan influence.

The Victorians found no difficulty in selecting the best-loved and most attractive of these traditions, and absorbing them into their newly sanitized, family-style Christmas. The house would be decked with greenery – holly, ivy and mistletoe artistically arranged over windows, doors, pictures and fireplaces. And, hanging between the evergreens, mottoes picked out in tiny flowers and bordered with mosses. Candles were arranged in heavy silver candlesticks to light the rooms, with smaller candles on the Christmas tree. Their pagan origins and rituals conveniently forgotten, the greenery and candles remained. A century later, they are to us equally symbolic of the traditional Victorian Christmas.

While Grandmother knits, and watches the pot, the children have been out collecting holly, ivy and mistletoe – and the traditional Yule log. These Christmas customs date back to pagan times symbolizing fertility and ensuring good luck in the coming year.

$\mathscr{S}$HIMMERING BOWS

These versatile bows look wonderful supporting leafy swags of dark green ivy or garlands of holly and spruce, sparkling with glass baubles.

Materials

16in (40cm) of twisted paper ribbon
Matching threads
1¾yd (1.5m) of lace, ⅝in (15mm) wide
1yd (90cm) of sheer striped ribbon, 1in (2.5cm) wide
Tiny glass bauble
Clear adhesive
8in (20cm) stem wire (or thin wire)

Order of work

FOR ONE BOW

1. Open out the paper ribbon. Fold in half to find the centre, then gather across the centre tightly by binding with thread.

2. Turn the cut ends to the back, gathering and binding them behind the centre, overlapping the ends ½in (1cm).

3. Stitch lace neatly along both edges of a 16in (40cm) length of the sheer ribbon. Gather across the centre of the ribbon, then bind it to the centre of the paper bow. Take the ends smoothly around to the back of the bow. Gather the cut ends and stitch them to the back of the bow.

4. Stitch lace along both edges of a 10in (25cm) length of sheer ribbon. Gather across the centre, then fold the ribbon. Fix the ribbon tails under the bow.

5. Join the cut ends of an 8in (20cm) length of sheer ribbon. Gather one straight edge and draw up to form a rosette, leaving a hole in the middle

Swags and garlands make elegant decorations but make sure that greenery is hung well away from open fires.

large enough to take the stem of the bauble.

6. Stitch the cut ends of an 8in (20cm) length of lace. Gather the straight edge and draw up to form a rosette, leaving a hole in the middle.

7. Fit the bauble through the lace and then the ribbon rosettes, gluing it from the back to hold. Glue the

rosettes to the middle of the bow.

8. Bend a piece of wire into a U-shape then almost open it flat again. Work tiny oversewing stitches over the middle of the wire to attach it to the back of the bow. The bow is secured to swags or garlands by twisting the wire ends together. Clip the wire ends shorter if desired.

MAKING MOCK BOWS

1. Mark the centre close to the lower edge. Decide the finished bow width, halve the measurement and mark points X, this distance from the centre, close to the top edge.

2. Pass a needle and thread, from the back through the centre point. Bring the ribbon ends around and pass the needle through points X at the front.

3. Draw up the bow, pulling it into shape.

4. Bind the centre of the bow tightly with the thread end.

CANDLELIGHT FOR CHRISTMAS

*For Victorian ambience, plain Venetian
candles need nothing more than a
decorated stand to set them off.*

Materials

RIBBONS, LACE AND PEARLS

Thin cardboard
Three stands, about 2½in (6cm)
   diameter
Clear adhesive
Reel of olive green gift-tie ribbon, ¾in
   (18mm) wide
1⅛yd (1m) cream guipure lace, ⅜in
   (9mm) deep
Three 5in (12.5cm)-long mulberry-
   coloured Venetian candles
Pearl beads
White sewing thread

Order of work

1. FOR EACH CANDLE Cut a strip of cardboard a little narrower than the ribbon, and about ⅜in (1cm) longer than the circumference of the stand. Fit it around the stand and glue the join.
2. Wrap ribbon around the cardboard and overlap and glue the join. Cut another strip of ribbon and fit it inside, so that it lies flat against the cardboard. Glue lace around the outside.
3. Cut a 1½in (4cm)-diameter circle of cardboard and cut a hole in the centre to fit the candle. Push the candle through it and into the stand.
4. Trace the leaf shape onto thin cardboard and cut it out for a template. Cut fourteen ribbon leaves.
5. Glue seven leaves, evenly spaced,

around the cardboard circle. Then glue the remaining leaves on top, between the first ones.
6. Glue lace around the base of the candle. Thread pearls on white thread and knot into a circlet to surround the lace.

Materials

RIBBONS AND ROSES

1¾yd (1.5m) sheer striped (or tartan
   taffeta) ribbon 1in (2.5cm) wide
1¾yd (1.5m) gold-edged satin
   ribbon, ⅝in (15mm) wide
Matching sewing thread
Pieces of plastic adhesive (the type
   that can be kneaded into shape)
A stand about 2½in (6cm) in diameter
8in (20cm)-long Venetian candle

Order of work

1. FOR EACH CANDLE Cut the striped (or tartan) ribbon into five 10in (25cm) lengths.
2. Make each into a 5⅛in (13cm)-wide mock bow. (Refer to page 17 for making a mock bow.)
3. Cut the gold-edged ribbon into five 12in (30cm) lengths. Form these into ribbon roses. Sew the roses securely to the centre of the bows. Bind a small lump of adhesive at the centre back of the bow before securing the thread end.
4. Fix the bows, equally spaced, around the stand. Insert the candle.

Trace this pattern

*RIGHT: Taffeta, tartan,
satin, stripes and gift-tie
ribbons are used in different
ways. Colour schemes should
either tone or contrast with the
candle, creating a carefully
integrated effect.*

MAKING RIBBON ROSES

1. Fold the ribbon end diagonally.

2. Make a small fold at the corner.

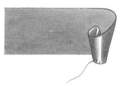

3. Roll the ribbon from the end, hold with small stitches.

4. Fold the ribbon diagonally towards you.

5. Roll until the ribbon is straight, stitch again.

6. Continue, folding, rolling and stitching.

CHRISTMAS WREATH

*Ever since Roman times, wreaths and
garlands have been used to decorate the
home in December, signifying re-growth
and good times to come.*

Materials

Gold paint
8 fir cones
Dried willow (or grapevine) wreath
Trails of fresh ivy
A few ivy leaves
Sprigs of holly
Sprigs of greenery, larch, fir, pine etc
3½yd (4m) approximately of gold-
   edged, red satin ribbon, 9mm
   (⅜in) wide
Sprigs of artificial holly berries
Small gold beads
No. 20 florist's stem wires, 8–10in
   (20–25cm) long

Order of work

1. Paint the fir cones with gold paint
and leave to dry.
2. Push one end of a stem wire
between the lowest seeds of the cone
leaving about 1½in (4cm) of the short
end protruding. Tightly wind the
wire around and through the cone
seeds to meet the short end. Twist the
ends together. Bend the wire so that it
is on the underside of the cone. Trim
the ends to the same length, leaving
two 'legs'.
3. Attach wires to the sprigs of holly,
ivy and other greenery. Twist a wire
around the sprigs stems, leaving two
'legs'.
4. Make eight mock bows from the
ribbon (refer to page 17 for making

mock bows). Twist wire round the
middle of the bows leaving two 'legs'.
5. Glue 3in (7.5cm) pieces of wire to
the gold beads. Twist the stems of
artificial berries with the gold bead
wire, then twist them around the
middle of the bows.
6. Wind trails of ivy round the
wreath, letting them fall naturally
between the willow strands.
7. Insert the mounted sprigs of holly
around the outside edges of the
wreath, twisting the wire 'legs'
together at the back. Fill in spaces
with ivy sprigs and sprigs of
greenery. Do not over-fill the wreath
– it will look better if some of the
willow strands show through.
8. Fasten the gold-painted pine cones
into position, spacing them around
the wreath. Attach the ribbon bows.
9. Tie the remaining ribbon to the top
of the wreath for a hanger.

Bend one end of the wire
round the sprig stem to make
the 'legs'.

Pass the wire between the
cone seeds, leaving a short
end.

Twist the wire ends together
under the cone to make two
'legs'.

*Use fresh or dried material to
make festive willow wreaths.
Glittering ribbons and tiny
glass baubles can be added for
sparkle.*

CHAPTER TWO

Thou and I shalt see him dine...

THE CHRISTMAS FEAST

THE VICTORIAN CHRISTMAS DINNER WAS NOT UNLIKE THE ONE THAT WE ENJOY TODAY, THOUGH A FAT GOOSE OR CAPON WAS MORE COMMON THAN TURKEY, AND THE PUDDING WAS LIKE A HEAVILY FRUITED CANNON BALL, STEAMED IN THE WASH BOILER. THE TRADITIONAL FARE HAD GRADUALLY EVOLVED DOWN THE CENTURIES, FROM THE DAYS WHEN A DECORATED BOAR'S HEAD WAS CEREMONIALLY CARRIED IN PROCESSION HERALDED BY TRUMPETS, A SWAN GRACED THE TOP TABLE, AND PLUM PUDDING WAS A FRUITY MUTTON SOUP.

The Grocers'! oh, the Grocers'! ... the blended scents of tea and coffee were so grateful to the nose ... the raisins were so plentiful and rare, the almonds so extremely white, the sticks of cinnamon so long and straight, the other spices so delicious, the candied fruits so caked and spotted with molten sugar as to make the coldest lookers-on feel faint, and subsequently bilious. Nor was it that the figs were moist and pulpy, or that the French plums blushed in modest tartness from their highly-decorated boxes, or that everything was good to eat and in its Christmas dress...

From *A Christmas Carol* by Charles Dickens

*I*n earlier centuries, when Christmas owed more to traditional pagan festivals than to Christianity, the medieval celebrations centred around a magnificently decorated boar's head. Surrounded by winter greenery and herbs, with an apple or orange stuck between its teeth, it was ceremoniously carried in on a silver platter, often accompanied by trumpeters and a choir. In fact, Queen Victoria still observed this ancient custom, although the typical English Victorian Christmas feast was much closer to the traditional one that we enjoy today. But it still retained something of its pagan origins.

For the better-off, a fat goose, a capon or a side of beef was the favourite choice for Christmas dinner. For poor people, it was more likely to be a tasty rabbit – especially in country areas, where it came free, as would a very special luxury, blackbird pie. Poorer people had not the facilities to roast a goose or a piece of meat anyway and most people took their dinner to the baker,

where his bread oven was put to good use on Christmas morning. At dinner-time the streets were full of hurrying people and appetizing smells, as the precious load was carried home in happy anticipation.

Turkeys, although available, became popular only towards the end of the century. The bird originally arrived in England from America in the mid-sixteenth century when a swan had been considered the ultimate bird for a great feast. But the turkey soon began to replace it, although at the end of the eighteenth century, turkey still remained a luxury that only the very rich could afford, which made it the supreme status symbol for Christmas dinner!

Although still expensive, the turkey became more generally obtainable in the nineteenth century. This is seen in Charles Dickens' story, *A Christmas Carol*. Scrooge dreams that he sees Bob Cratchit's family making the most of a small goose for their Christmas dinner. So, when he wakes to find that it is still only Christmas morning, he sends a

In The Christmas Hamper, *by Robert Braithwaite Martineau, the family gathers round to admire the fine turkey, which has just arrived. Goose had been the most popular bird for the Christmas feast, and was gradually replaced by the turkey.*

boy to buy a prize turkey for the family. It was not until the end of the century – and Victoria's reign – that the roast turkey was firmly established, served with bacon, sausages, stuffings of different kinds, forcemeat and gravy, accompanied by roast potatoes, brussels sprouts, cabbage, turnips and bread sauce.

The English Plum Pudding, served at the end of a Victorian Christmas feast, was directly descended from the Christmas feast of earlier centuries. The basic Christmas Pudding recipe still used today has an intriguing history. Before the mid-seventeenth century plum-porridge or plum-pottage resembled a thick soup, and was served with the meat course and eaten with a spoon. It was originally made by the Celts, and was a spiced mixture of hulled wheat boiled in milk, called frumenty. Later it was made from mutton and beef boiled in broth, with breadcrumbs, raisins and prunes, wine, spices, ginger and cloves. However, around the time that the stiffer mixture became popular, Puritan Oliver Cromwell declared plum pudding illegal, and anyone caught making or eating it was liable to be fined and sent to prison. But the plum pudding survived – and by the nineteenth century was much as it is known today.

ABOVE LEFT: The pudding was prepared well before Christmas, then tied in a cloth and gently lowered into the washboiler. There it was boiled for several hours, filling the house with its tantilizingly delicious aroma.

LEFT: Children of the upper and middle-class families usually had their meals in the nursery. But at Christmas, which Victorians regarded as a children's festival, they were allowed to sit up at the table.

Christmas is coming
And the geese are getting
    fat,
Please put a penny in the
    old man's hat,
If you haven't got a penny,
A ha'penny will do,
If you haven't got a
    ha'penny -
God bless you!

Old rhyme

Although English winters were sometimes mild, Victorian artists drew Christmas with snow and ice outside and a roaring fire, rich food and drink indoors.

Preparations for making the pudding would begin well before Christmas. When all the ingredients had been combined together in a big bowl, everyone had to have a stir 'for luck' (although this superstition might well have been the device of a wily cook, for stirring the heavy mixture was – and still is – exhausting work!). Finally, a set of silver charms or tiny silver coins would be added – to await the lucky finders when the pudding was served.

The heavily fruited suet mixture was tied in a cloth and cooked for hours – in the wash boiler if there was nothing else large enough to hold it. On Christmas Day, after several more hours cooking, the rich, dark, cannon ball shape, with its heady aroma of fruit, candied peel, spice and spirits, was set on the plate and topped with a sprig of holly. Just before serving it was drenched in brandy, then set alight and carried flaming to the table, to be greeted with cheers and laughter. Port followed the meal, and, for those who still had room for more, Stilton

cheese, fresh fruit, roast chestnuts, almonds and raisins, walnuts, sugar plums and chocolate truffles.

However, in the mid-nineteenth century, it was only the lucky few who could expect a special Christmas dinner. The machines of the Industrial Revolution that had created the well-to-do middle class had also created a depth of poverty never previously experienced. Before they migrated to the towns to find work in the factories, even the poorest country-dweller could manage to be fairly self-sufficient with what he grew in his cottage garden. But huddled together in insanitary, back-to-back houses, wearing thin, ragged clothes and without coal for a fire, the poor had little reason to celebrate Christmas. Nor anything to celebrate it with. Those in work toiled long hours for little pay: the unemployed had to beg. Drink was their only consolation, and what little money they had was often exchanged for a few hours of escape into oblivion.

The idea of Christmas as a family celebration was invented by the

Victorians, with the direct object of arousing a new sense of morality and social awareness. The Queen and her husband, Prince Albert, with their passionate enthusiasm for home and family, reflected this in their own life.

The Industrial Revolution had bridged the great divide between the upper and lower classes. The new middle class had worked hard to achieve their prosperity which bought them comfortable homes, servants, fashionable clothes and plenty of leisure. But it gave them something else: social status. To advance it, they naturally sought to emulate those above them – and the Royal Family was the ultimate role model.

As it happened, they couldn't have had a better one. The Victorian media was a helpful contributory factor. Newspapers and periodicals showing scenes of cosy domesticity – the royal mama and papa surrounded by up to nine children, all demurely clean, neat and well-behaved – provided a perfect example.

Conscious of their enviable lifestyle, the better-off now saw their role as benefactors. The popular author, Charles Dickens, was a considerable influence. *A Christmas Carol*, originally published in 1843, was a deliberate tear-jerker inspired by the poverty he saw among factory workers in the industrial cities. Dickens' sentimental tale reached a wide audience on both sides of the Atlantic, and made his readers aware of how the other half lived.

The Victorians came to see Christmas as a special time for charity. Baskets of food and warm clothing were graciously handed over to the poor – and gratefully received. Funds were raised to ensure that those in workhouses, prisons, reformatories and other institutions received presents of oranges, tobacco and sweets, and enjoyed a hearty meal of roast beef and plum pudding ... a treat that was beyond the means of ordinary working-class families.

Once their social conscience had been eased, the English Victorian middle and upper classes were free to indulge, cared for by a hard-working domestic staff who had spent many hours preparing for this special day. They, of course, could not expect to spend a holiday with their own families. However, they probably enjoyed much better Christmas fare where they were, despite spending their long working day in a below-ground kitchen.

In Charles Dickens' tale of the miser who meets the spirits of Christmas Past, Present and Future, Scrooge's third visitor is a jolly giant with a throne of turkeys, geese, game, poultry, sucking pigs, sausages, mince pies, plum-puddings, oysters, chestnuts, fruit, cakes and bowls of punch.

$\mathcal{T}$HE TRADITIONAL FEAST

Whether your choice is turkey or goose you can make it an authentic Victorian Christmas with delicious accompaniments.

The boar's head of the medieval feasts was not entirely forgotten by the English Victorians. It probably appealed to their love of realism on the table, for they delighted in reassembling roasted birds or animals with their tail feathers, heads and eyes in place before they were brought to the dining room. At Christmas-time, a pig's head would be cooked in aspic, then artistically decorated with egg-white, prunes, colourful sliced vegetables, parsley, peppercorns, lemon peel and almonds. Crowned with a holly wreath, it made a spectacular centrepiece.

Forcemeat stuffing should be put into the bird immediately before cooking, or rolled into balls and sautéd in butter.

CHESTNUT FORCEMEAT

Ingredients

1lb (500g) Chestnuts

½ pint (300ml/1¼ cups) Milk

2oz (50g/¼ cup) Butter

3oz (75g/1½ cups) fresh white Breadcrumbs

8oz (250g) good quality Sausage meat

2 tblsp (30ml) chopped, fresh Parsley

1 tblsp (15ml) chopped, fresh Sage

Pinch of ground Mace

1 Turkey liver, chopped

Salt and Pepper

Method

1. Shell the chestnuts by cutting a cross in the top of each, then bake in an oven at 190°C (375°F/Gas 5) for 20 minutes. Remove the outer and inner skins.
2. Place the shelled chestnuts in a pan with just enough milk to cover. Bring to the boil and allow to simmer slowly until the nuts are tender and the liquid is absorbed.
3. Mash coarsely and add the butter and breadcrumbs, and mix with the sausage meat, parsley, sage, mace, turkey liver and seasonings.
4. Use the forcemeat to stuff a 10lb (4.5kg) turkey or goose. Or roll into balls and sauté in butter until brown.

Serves: about 9

GLAZED CARROTS AND TURNIPS

Ingredients

2lb (1kg) Carrots, peeled and cut across and in half lengthways

2lb (1kg) Turnips, peeled and quartered

4oz (125g/½ cup) Butter

1 pint (600ml/2½ cups) freshly-made Chicken stock

Large pinch of ground Mace

Salt and Pepper

Caster (superfine) Sugar

Method

1. Place the carrots and turnips in a pan. Cover with water and add salt. Bring to the boil and simmer gently for 5–6 minutes. Drain.

2. In a large, deep frying pan, melt the butter and then add the carrots and turnips, seasoning, and a large pinch of sugar.

3. Pour in the stock to come halfway up the pan, and cover with greased paper and a lid.

4. Cook gently until tender. Remove the carrots and turnips and reduce the stock rapidly to a thin glaze. Return the vegetables to the pan and coat them well. Serve.

Serves: 8

CRANBERRY AND APPLE SAUCE

Ingredients

1lb (500g) fresh Cranberries, washed

2 cooking Apples, peeled, cored and chopped

8fl oz (250ml/1 cup) Water

4oz (125g/¾ cup) brown Sugar

3fl oz (90ml/⅓ cup) Port

1 tblsp (15ml) of Red Currant Jelly

Method

1. Place the cranberries and apple in a saucepan. Bruise the cranberries slightly with the back of a wooden spoon. Add the water. Bring to the boil and simmer for about 15 minutes or until the fruit is softened.

2. Add the sugar, port and redcurrant jelly. Cook to melt the sugar and remove from the heat.

3. Serve cold in a glass dish.

Serves: 6-8

TOP: *Glistening under the lights, glazed vegetables look and taste delicious.*

ABOVE: *Sweet-sour sauce made from cranberries is delicious with turkey, poultry, duck and pork.*

Brandy butter is the perfect accompaniment to plum pudding. Any left-over butter can be used up on hot mince pies as an after-Christmas treat.

BRANDY BUTTER
— ❅ —

Ingredients

6oz (175g/ ¾cup) unsalted Butter,
   softened

¼tsp (1.25ml) ground Nutmeg

¼tsp (1.25ml) grated Lemon zest

12oz (375g/3 cups) Icing (confectioner's)
   Sugar (sifted)

2-3 tblsp (10–15ml) Brandy

Method

1. Beat the butter until soft, then beat in the nutmeg and lemon zest gradually.
2. Add the sugar with the brandy, beating well after each addition.
3. Mound into dishes or roll into walnut-sized balls.

Serves: 6–8

Plum pudding makes a filling end to a heavy meal: even more so when it is further enriched at the table with brandy butter and thick cream. Few can resist this traditional finish to the English Christmas dinner, even though common sense tells them that they should prefer something lighter!

In a Victorian household, leftover pudding was never wasted. One favourite was to fry it in butter and serve it topped with sugar or rum butter. Another was to moisten the crumbled pudding with brandy, then seal it in a pastry crust. Small, pre-cooked pastry tartlets were sometimes filled with crumbled, brandy-moistened pudding then topped with a swirl of meringue and baked. And, for a Christmas version of bread-and-butter pudding, the remaining pudding was cut into wedges and piled into a dish, an egg custard poured over the top and then baked.

PLUM PUDDING
— ❄ —
Ingredients

4oz (125g/1 cup) plain (all-purpose)
  Flour

4oz (125g/2 cups) fresh white
  Breadcrumbs

4oz (125g) Suet (optional)

8oz (250g/1⅓ cups) dark brown Sugar

6oz (175g/2 cups) Sultanas (golden
  raisins)

6oz (175g/2 cups) Raisins

4oz (125g/¾ cup) Candied peel, chopped

6oz (175g/2¼ cups) Currants

4oz (125g/1 cup) whole blanched Almonds,
  chopped

Grated rind of 1 Lemon and 1 small
  Orange

1 Carrot, peeled and grated

1 tsp (5ml) mixed Spice

½ tsp (2.5ml) Salt

½ tsp (2.5ml) Bicarbonate of Soda

Juice of 1 Lemon and 1 Orange

4oz (125g/⅔ cup) Marmalade

6 medium-sized Eggs, beaten

2 fl oz (60ml/¼ cup) Stout

2 fl oz (60ml/¼ cup) Rum (optional)

2 fl oz (60ml/¼ cup) Brandy (optional)

Method

1. Mix all the dry ingredients together.

2. Make a well in the middle, add the juices, marmalade and eggs and stir in some of the dry ingredients.

3. Pour the stout into the centre of the other ingredients.

4. Mix well and beat for a few minutes.

5. Leave over night for the flavour to develop.

6. Divide the mixture in half. Place each amount in the centre of a doubled, well-floured 18 x 18in (46 x 46cm) square of muslin (fine cotton) fabric. Mould into neat rounds.

7. Draw up the edges of muslin and tie with thick string, allowing room for the pudding to expand.

8. Tie each pudding to a wooden spoon, and rest them over a large pan of boiling water.

9. Tightly cover the pan with foil and secure with string. Cook for approximately six hours, topping the pan up with boiling water if necessary.

10. Hang the puddings in a cool place until quite dry. Overwrap in foil and keep in a cool, dry place for several weeks.

TO SERVE: Remove the foil and cook as before for about two hours. Just before serving, pour a wine glass of rum or brandy over the pudding and set alight.

Serves: about 10

Richly fruited plum puddings can be stored, wrapped in cling film and foil, for 12 months or longer.

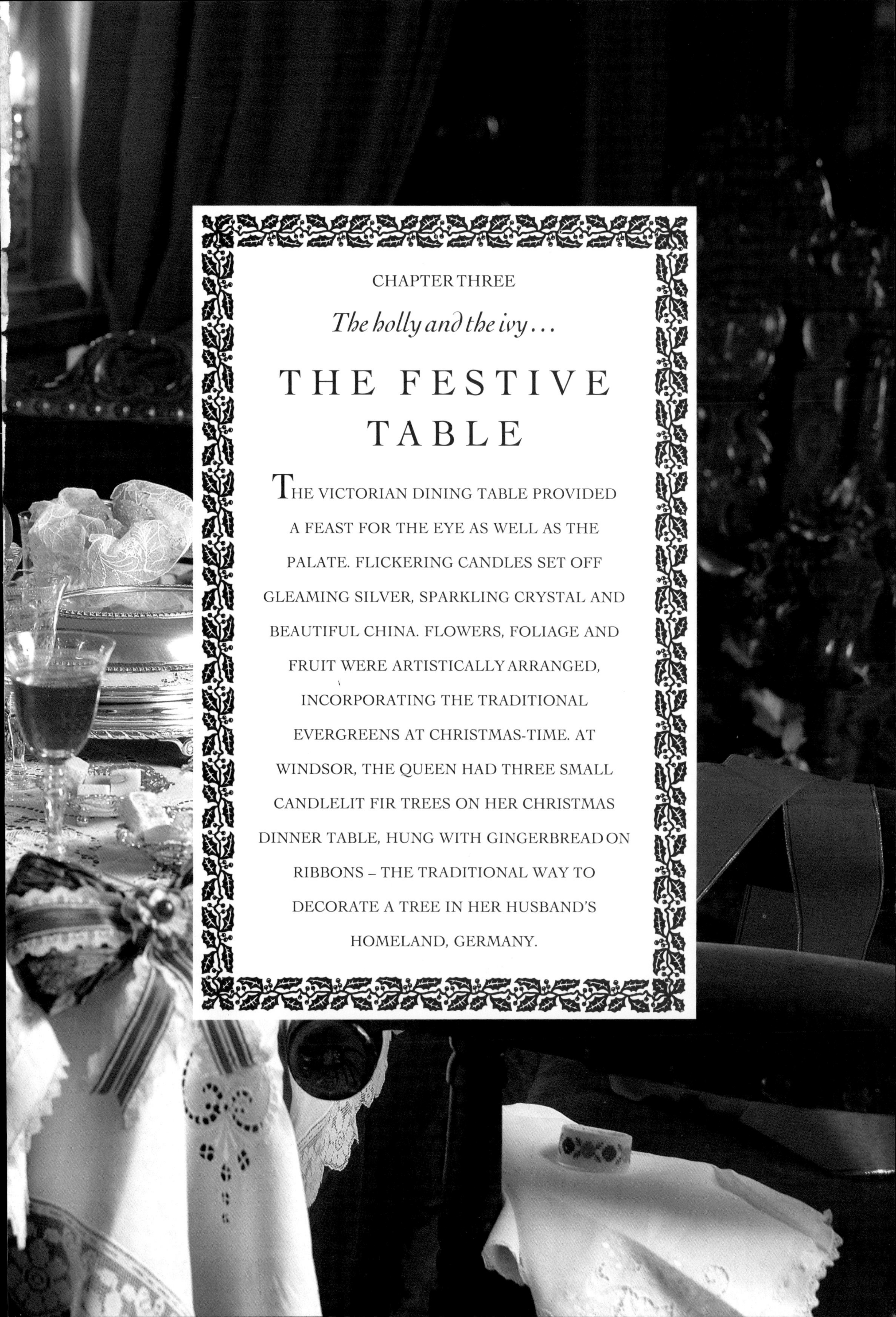

CHAPTER THREE

The holly and the ivy…

THE FESTIVE TABLE

THE VICTORIAN DINING TABLE PROVIDED

A FEAST FOR THE EYE AS WELL AS THE

PALATE. FLICKERING CANDLES SET OFF

GLEAMING SILVER, SPARKLING CRYSTAL AND

BEAUTIFUL CHINA. FLOWERS, FOLIAGE AND

FRUIT WERE ARTISTICALLY ARRANGED,

INCORPORATING THE TRADITIONAL

EVERGREENS AT CHRISTMAS-TIME. AT

WINDSOR, THE QUEEN HAD THREE SMALL

CANDLELIT FIR TREES ON HER CHRISTMAS

DINNER TABLE, HUNG WITH GINGERBREAD ON

RIBBONS – THE TRADITIONAL WAY TO

DECORATE A TREE IN HER HUSBAND'S

HOMELAND, GERMANY.

In England, a Victorian dinner party was an excuse to entertain and impress with an extravagant menu of attractively presented food – further enhanced by the artistic setting in which it was served. As much forethought and imagination went into planning the table decorations as the menu itself, and the gardener was as deeply involved in the discussions and preparations as the cook.

Until the 1850s, all the food had been set out on the table itself, and the plates and dishes were not cleared until the end of the meal. But the new continental fashion of dining *à la russe* left the dining table clear for spectacular arrangements of plants, flowers and fruit.

The grander the home, the more magnificent the table – each hostess determined to outdo her rivals. The dining room of a big house on the night of a special dinner party or ball was a breathtaking sight. A long table, smoothly covered by an immaculate white damask cloth would be set with sparkling crystal and fine china, often exquisitely patterned. Heavy velvet curtains covered the sash windows, with gas lamps lighting the scene, supplemented by a succession of branched candlesticks on the table, the flickering candles reflected in the highly polished silver and delicate wineglasses.

Tall fruit stands laden with plums, peaches, oranges, melons, apples and pears had leafy bunches of grapes spilling over the edge of each tier, the top one crowned with a magnificent pineapple surrounded by more fruit on a bed of greenery. Or the same selection of fruits would be arranged in an enormous silver basket, topped with a bunch of sugar-encrusted frosted grapes. The decorations became more and more adventurous, with mountains of fruit piled dangerously high between a shrubbery of pot plants beneath garlands of flowers and leafy arches. The sides of the cloth were sometimes swagged, held up with posies of flowers.

The food was brought to the table by the servants only as it was required. There would be tureens of clear consommé and thick soup. Roasts, meat dishes and poultry stood on the solid mahogany sideboard. Hors d'oeuvres and elaborately prepared entrées of fish, meat, poultry and eggs, with accompanying salads and vegetables, might be served from a dinner wagon. And on a side table an array of mouth-watering creamy confections – beautifully decorated fruit jellies, meringues, tarts, trifles, gateaux, tipsy cake, savarins, babas and similar desserts awaited their moment of glory.

Fresh foliage came from the greenhouse or conservatory, for the English Victorians were keen indoor gardeners. Ferns were much in demand, especially the maidenhair, its delicate fronds spreading out over

A massive table centre piled high with fruit and decorated with greenery was the mark of an elegant dinner party. The delicate leafy decoration was repeated on the serving dishes, surrounding the base.

the snowy white cloth, or providing misty greenery among the floral arrangements. Fern was even used to decorate food, surrounding shimmering jellies in translucent fruity colours or pale blancmanges scattered with scarlet geraniums or orange nasturtium petals.

Trailing smilax was another favourite, linking individual corner arrangements to a central one, or looped around the sides of the table between the guests. Pieces of dry, brown bracken made a stronger impact, as did trailing ivy, its shiny dark green leaves contrasting boldly with the pristine white and silver. At Christmas-time it was particularly appropriate, when it might have been combined with its traditional partner, holly.

Queen Victoria's enthusiasm for the decorated Christmas tree extended to having three small ones hung with gingerbread on the dining table, which was piled high with food, with an immense side of beef on the sideboard. On Christmas Day

the candles were lighted when dessert was served, and again on New Year's Day and Twelfth Night.

Towards the end of the century, a popular ladies' magazine was encouraging women to pay as much attention to their table decorations for Christmas as they did at other seasons of the year. The magazine suggested creating a 'lake' made from a narrow strip of looking-glass down the centre of the table, studded with islands of greenery and tiny trees.

In the latter half of the 19th century, dinner à la Russe became fashionable, where each course was brought to the table separately. The earlier system, dinner à la Française had meant that all the dishes were on the table at the same time.

In 1840, a London confectioner named Tom Smith conceived something that was to become a traditional English Christmas table decoration. During a business trip to France he had come across sugared almonds prettily wrapped in paper, twisted at each end. Bon-bons, as the sweets were called, were sold unwrapped in England, and Tom Smith saw this as an eye-catching way to market his products.

Legend has it that, as Tom Smith sat in front of the fire, the crack of a spark from a burning log provided the inspiration that he needed to give his bon-bons

more impact. He experimented with saltpetre and found that when a friction strip was inserted in the bon-bon – it broke in half with a bang when pulled at both ends. He emphasized the party mood by adding amusing paper hats and tiny trinkets.

So the 'cracker' literally exploded onto the Victorian scene, where it created such a sensation that it soon became an essential part of the Christmas festivities. The paper novelties continued to be called 'bon-bons' until the early 1920s when the term 'cracker' began to be more widely used.

*F*ESTIVE PLACE
SETTINGS

Cross stitch place settings with traditional themes bring nineteenth century elegance to today's dining tables.

⋊❄⋉

Materials

IVY TRAIL
For one place setting.
Graph paper
Piece of deep cream Aida evenweave
 fabric, 21 x 10in (52.5 x 25cm),
 with sixteen blocks to 1in (2.5cm)
Stranded embroidery cotton (floss)
 in the colours on the chart
Fusible tape
Heavyweight, non-woven
 interfacing (twice the size of each
 mat (optional) plus the napkin
 ring)
Fusible interfacing
Matching sewing thread
Clear adhesive

Note: for two place settings, allow
 10in (25cm) of 44in (110cm)-wide
 fabric. For four place settings you
 will need 20in (50cm) of 44in
 (110cm)-wide fabric.

Order of work

1. From the fabric, cut the place mat 16 x 10in (40 x 25cm) and the coaster 6in (15cm) square. Cut the fabric for the napkin ring 6 x 4in (15 x 10cm).
2. Working from the chart, plan out the complete design on graph paper, adding pairs of leaves at the points indicated. The place mat has eight leaves (four pairs) across both the top and bottom, and six leaves (three pairs) down each side. The coaster

has three leaves forming a corner, with a third leaf added to form the square. The napkin ring has a pair of leaves between shaded borders.
3. Outline the shapes in pencil, counting the squares, so that you have an accurate plan of the whole piece you are going to work. This will enable you to calculate where to place the design on the fabric.
4. Counting squares across the top and down one side, mark the centre of the design on your graph paper chart. Find the centre of your fabric by folding it in half twice and mark it with basting stitches.
5. Decide where you want to begin stitching and count the number of squares from the centre of your graph paper chart to that point. Count the corresponding number of blocks of threads on the fabric to your starting point.
6. Work the embroidery in cross stitch using two strands of cotton (floss) throughout and following the colour key. When the embroidery is finished, press the back of the work under a damp cloth.

Making up the Place Mat

7. For a quick and easy-to-wash mat, turn under a 1in (2.5cm) hem all round and fix it with fusible tape. Mitre the corners. Alternatively, you can draw threads for a hem-stitched fringed edge.

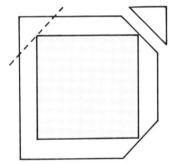

To mitre corners, mark the corner diagonally then trim it off. The cut edges are then brought together, narrow hems turned, and sewn together.

8. For a stiffened, heat-resistant mat, work as follows: trim the edges of the embroidery to leave an equal border of fabric all round.

9. Mark two pieces of fusible interfacing to the required size of the finished mat. Cut out the pieces of fusible interfacing.

10. Iron each piece of fusible interfacing onto the heavyweight interfacing and cut the edges level.

11. Place the embroidery right side down, remove the backing paper from one piece of heavyweight interfacing and position it on the embroidery, bonded side down. Iron it to bond, using a damp cloth.

12. Mitre the corners, then turn the raw edges over to the back, using fusible tape to fix them into place. Remove the backing paper from the second piece of heavyweight interfacing and iron it onto the back of the mat. Seal and neaten the corners with clear adhesive.

Making up the Napkin Ring

13. On fusible interfacing, draw a 6in (15cm)-long strip to the required width of the ring. Iron it onto heavyweight interfacing and cut out.

14. Place the trimmed embroidery face down. Bond the strip to the back of the embroidery so that the embroidery is centred.

15. Trim the long edges of the embroidered fabric, leaving a surplus at each side equal to the width of the interfacing, less ¼in (6mm).

16. Fold one edge over and fix it in place with fusible tape. Fold and fix the other long edge in the same way.

17. Trim the short ends neatly and overlap them. Secure with a touch of adhesive and sew the join.

Making up the Coaster

18. Finish the coaster as you did for the place mat.

Ivy evokes a Victorian table decoration for this three-piece place setting. The rich colours are typical of the period, dark green ivy contrasted with a warm border shading out to the colour of vintage claret. An elegant design that will grace your table for any special occasion.

Glistening baubles made by Bohemian glass-blowers were immensely popular from the 1870s on, and are still a favourite tree decoration. They inspired the simple design for this special Christmas place setting of jewel-coloured balls shining between sprigs of dark green spruce.

Materials

CHRISTMAS TREE BAUBLES
For one place setting
Graph paper
Piece of cream-coloured Aida evenweave fabric, 21 x 10in (52.5 x 25cm) with sixteen blocks to 1in (2.5cm)
Stranded embroidery cotton (floss) in the colours on the chart
Fusible interfacing (twice the size of the mat (optional) plus the napkin ring)
Heavyweight, sew-in, non-woven interfacing (twice the size of the mat (optional) plus the napkin ring)
Fusible tape
Matching sewing thread
Clear adhesive

Note: For fabric for two or four place settings, refer to the note on page 36 for the Ivy Trail place setting.

Order of work

1. From the fabric, cut the place mat 16 x 10in (40 x 25cm) and the coaster 6in (15cm) square. Cut the napkin ring 6 x 4in (15 x 10cm).
2. Working from the chart, plan out the complete design on graph paper repeating the six colours in sequence. The mat has nineteen balls across the top and bottom and thirteen down each side, arranged so that there is a red ball at each corner. The complete design for the coaster is shown on the chart: note the position of the highlights on this when working the place mat. The napkin ring is a line of balls, following the colour sequence so that a red one falls in the centre.
3. Outline the shapes in pencil, counting the squares carefully, so that you have an accurate plan of the whole piece that you are going to work. Work the detail of the embroidery from the chart.
4. Counting squares across the top and down one side, mark the centre of your graph paper chart. Find the centre of your fabric by folding it in half then in half again, and mark the centre with basting stitches.
5. Decide where you want to begin stitching and count the number of squares from the centre of the graph paper chart to that point. Count the corresponding number of blocks of threads on the fabric to your starting point.
6. Work the embroidery in cross stitch using two strands of cotton throughout and following the colour key. Use only one strand of green for the straight stitches forming the sprigs of fir.

Making up

7. Press the work. Make up the place mat, coaster and napkin ring as for the Ivy Trail place setting.

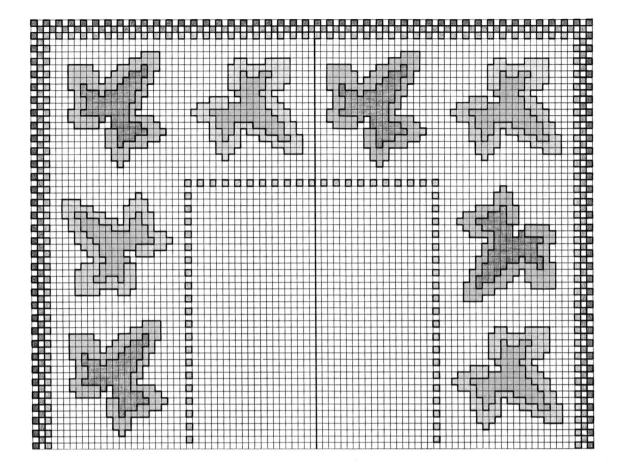

Ivy trail

DMC	ANCHOR
3345 Deep green	262
3346 Mid-leaf	266
3347 Light leaf	255
3688 Mid-pink	76
3687 Deep pink	77
3685 Wine	43

Christmas Tree Baubles

DMC	ANCHOR
321 Red	46
444 Yellow	290
552 Purple	98
783 Gold	307
3760 Blue	929
970 Orange	324
469 Mid-olive	267

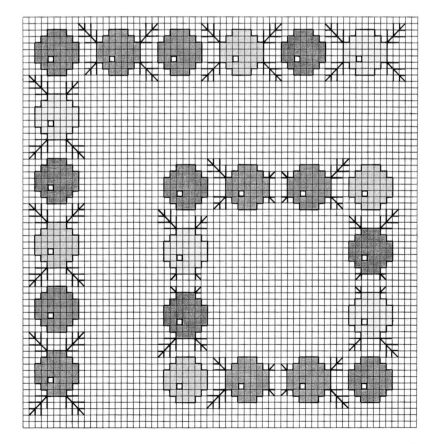

CHAPTER FOUR

The stars in the bright sky…

THE
CHRISTMAS
TREE

To the Victorians, a fir tree decorated with candles and ornaments was an enchanting novelty. In Germany, birthplace of Victoria's consort, Prince Albert, it was a centuries-old tradition, dating back to pre-Christian times. The queen fell in love with the idea – and Albert wanted everyone in his adopted country to share her delight in the magic of the Christmas tree. The candles and angel represent the Bethlehem starlit sky and the coming of the light of the world.

The origins of the Christmas tree are obscure, but probably evolved from a combination of German tree-worship and the pagan winter festivals, when evergreens were brought indoors to symbolize the continuation of life and growth.

The pagan Germans had worshipped trees – especially the oak – and in winter they hung colourful decorations on the bare branches to encourage the tree-spirits to return and produce fresh leaves. When Christianity was introduced they were anxious not to upset the tree-spirits by abandoning them. The fir tree was put forward as a suitable alternative, since its triangular shape suggested the Holy Trinity. The converted Germans were happy with this compromise, and the decorated fir tree became a popular Yuletide custom, dating back to the eighth and ninth centuries.

Eventually a small fir tree was brought indoors, but candles were added only in the middle of the seventeenth century – said to commemorate the starlit sky on the night of the Nativity, and to symbolize Christ as the Light of the World. Before that, the tree was hung with paper roses to honour Our Lady, with apples, wafers, gold-foil and sweet candies. On top was a golden-haired cherub representing the Christ-child, but by the time the Christmas tree reached England, this had become a protective angel dressed in gold.

Then it changed again, and by the end of the century a porcelain or wax doll dressed as a Christmas fairy topped the tree.

The adults stay up late on Christmas Eve, preparing to delight the children with paper chains, delicate cut-paper hangings, baubles, gingerbread and small gifts. Candles were fixed to the branches, to be lit only for a carefully supervised hour in the evening.

It is often thought that Queen Victoria's consort, Prince Albert, introduced the Christmas tree to Britain from his native Germany. In fact, the Prince Consort only popularized the custom in his adopted country. The decorated tree had been a Christmas feature at the royal court as early as 1800, when Queen Charlotte entertained local children at Queen's Lodge, Windsor. To their delight they found a yew tree set in an enormous tub in the middle of the room, alight with tiny wax candles. From its branches hung bunches of sweetmeats, almonds and raisins, all prettily wrapped in paper, with attractive fruits and small toys. Before they left, each child received a toy and a share of the edible decorations.

In later years Queen Adelaide, wife of King William IV, had an enormous tree set up every Christmas Eve, lit with tapers, hung with gilded apples, pears and walnuts, and bearing valuable gifts for her ladies and other guests.

The custom of sending Christmas cards developed slowly but surely. By the latter part of the century, it had become an art form in its own right, as illustrated by this superb example of printing and paper-cutting. The branches pull away from the centre to reveal children playing party games.

It has to be said that, charming as the candlelit tree may have been, it often ended in disaster. If left unattended, a falling wax candle could so easily catch a dry twig or decoration, and the whole tree would be ablaze. Or an excited child might brush against a branch, with the same tragic result. In the United States, in the 1880s the spring clip holder, which is still in use today, was invented. Although this reduces the danger considerably, there is still a risk of fire.

For safety's sake, most homes would have the tree lit for only an hour or so on Christmas Day. In wealthy establishments with a large staff, a footman or other servant was designated to keep watch over the tree and snuff the candles with a wet sponge fixed to a pole as they burnt down.

In the United States, in the 1880s, little electric 'fairy lights' were produced especially for Christmas trees and offered a safe alternative – although only for those well-to-do homes that were wired for electricity. Today we have the best of both worlds, with tiny electric 'candles' that, while appearing satisfyingly realistic, are entirely safe as long as normal safety procedures are observed.

Meanwhile, the young Princess Victoria described in her diary on Christmas Eve 1832, five years before her accession, the pair of trees, each set on a large round table, which her mother had prepared for the festivities at Kensington Palace. The trees were decorated with candles and sugar ornaments, and the presents were set around the base. The excited young princess found that one table was entirely for her!

The very first Christmas after Victoria's marriage to Prince Albert was spent at Windsor Castle, where the couple each had a tree set up in their own rooms, surrounded by gifts

Queen Victoria, Prince Albert and five of their children gathered around their candlelit tree at Windsor Castle in 1848. To the Prince Consort's delight, this picture was widely published, and did much to promote and establish the Christmas tree in both Great Britain and the United States.

ABOVE: A German mama decks the tree with the traditional gingerbread. Honey cakes were another favourite, rich in orange and lemon peel, almonds and mixed spices and spread with lemon icing.

'with which each took pleasure in surprising the other'. Christmas presents were unknown in England at this time, but it was the custom in the Prince Consort's homeland, Germany.

By 1847 the decorated fir tree had become a tradition. The royal children shared a tree. So did the ladies-in-waiting. Another tree was surrounded by presents for the members of the Royal Household, each bearing a card written by the Queen herself. But Queen Victoria, her mother and her consort each had their own. All were decorated with tinsel, candles, toffees and gingerbread. The candles were extinguished after the present-giving, and re-lit at dusk. There were three more small trees, with similar decorations, in the dining room.

Both the Queen and Prince Albert were anxious to demonstrate to her subjects the importance of a happy family life. The Prince Consort considered the Christmas tree epitomized the close and loving harmony of his own family; so he set about popularizing it in no uncertain way. He encouraged other members of the Royal Family to follow his example in presenting trees to barracks and schools, where children's parties were organized. Charming pictures appeared in the press showing the Royal Family gathered around a decorated tree, ablaze with tiny candles and laden with small gifts. In a surprisingly few years the Christmas tree had become generally adopted in British upper and middle-class homes.

It was inevitable that the custom should spread to America too, where so many European immigrants had settled, bringing with them their own traditions as well as the various arts and crafts of their respective countries. No doubt this artistic

inspiration resulted in American Christmas trees being even more imaginatively decorated than those of the more insular British. The colourful Pennsylvania Dutch (Deutsch) 'hex' designs from the Rhineland, the delicate painting of Hungary and Czechoslovakia and the cut paperwork of Bavarians – plus German gingerbread – all helped to create the enthusiasm for spectacularly dressed Christmas trees that are so popular in the United States today.

The Prince Consort began a small miracle with his fir tree. It achieved the Victorian 'family Christmas' that he dreamed of; but it also brought about a sense of community that has spread around the world.

By 1890 the tree had grown in size, and moved from table to floor. The candles perpetuated a centuries-old tradition, but paper-thin coloured glass baubles were introduced only in the 1870s. In Bohemia, where baubles originated, they were used by the superstitious to ward off 'the evil eye'.

*L*ACY BAUBLE

*A nostalgic decoration in the true Victorian
tradition of lace and flowers, lustrous velvet
and satin ribbons and tiny seed pearls.*

Materials

Petroleum Jelly
Smooth-surfaced ball,
    approximately 2½in (6cm) in
    diameter
Sheets of toilet tissue
Prepared wallpaper paste
Deep-toned soft-ply paper table
    napkins (or face tissues)
¼yd (23cm) lace, 1¼in (30mm) wide
Assorted pearl beads (to trim the
    base)
Fine wire
8in (20cm) satin ribbon, ¼in (6mm)
    wide
Tiny pins
12in (30cm) sheer striped ribbon, 1in
    (2.5cm) wide
12in (30cm) satin ribbon, ⅝in
    (15mm) wide
12in (30cm) velvet ribbon, ⅝in
    (15mm) wide
½yd (40cm) tiny pearl bead trimming
Dried or artificial flowers
Clear adhesive

Order of work

1. Smear a thick layer of petroleum jelly over the surface of the ball.
2. Cut sheets of toilet tissue into sixteen roughly even squares, and separate the plies. Cover the surface of the ball with slightly overlapping squares of the tissue.
3. Applying paste liberally, apply another overlapping layer of tissue squares all over the ball.
4. Apply three more layers, then leave the ball to dry in a warm place, turning it once. When completely dry, apply several more layers of tissue and leave until thoroughly dry.
5. Cut all round the paper shell using a sharp knife, marking it in two halves. Pencil a line across the cut at one point, so that you can match the halves again. Remove each half carefully from the ball.
6. Place the two halves together again and join them by pasting over the cut edges with more squares of tissue. Allow to dry.
7. Cut similar-sized squares of deep-toned tissue and paste three layers over the ball. Allow to dry thoroughly.
8. Trim off the top edge of the lace, then paste it round the ball. Allow the pasted lace to dry.
9. Push a thin, sharp skewer right through the centre of the ball, to make small holes at the top and bottom.
10. Select three or four graduated pearl beads for the bottom. Cut a 10in (25cm) length of wire. Thread the smallest bead onto the centre of the wire, then bend it in half and thread both ends through the remaining beads, in the correct order of size. Push the wire up through the holes in the ball until the beads are held close against the base.
11. Join the cut ends of the ¼in (6mm)-wide ribbon to make a hanging loop. Thread the wire ends through the ribbon loop. Wrap the wire round securely.

12. Cut the string of tiny pearl beads into four equal lengths. Bind the cut ends of each strand together to form a loop and fix to the top of the ball with pins, so that the loops hang evenly round it.

13. Cut the sheer ribbon into four equal lengths. Glue the cut ends of each together to form loops. Pin or glue the loops round the top of the ball, spacing them evenly.

14. Make more loops with the ⅝in (15mm)-wide satin ribbon and position them between the previous loops.

15. Form the velvet ribbon into a bow (see page 17) measuring 3½in (9cm) from the centre. Fix the bow on top, between the strands of the satin ribbon hanging loop. Wire or glue flower heads to the centre of the bow.

A child's ball is the basis for this exquisite papier mâché decoration.

MINIATURE WREATH

Quick and easy to make from natural materials, add Christmas charm in traditional colours with tartan ribbon and a shining silver bell or glass baubles.

Materials

Natural garden raffia
10in (25cm) of tartan taffeta ribbon, 1in (2.5cm) wide
¾yd (70cm) of green/red striped grosgrain ribbon, ⅛in (3mm) wide (or to tone with the tartan ribbon)
½yd (40cm) of scarlet single-face satin ribbon, ¼in (6mm) wide
4in (10cm) of scarlet satin ribbon, ¹⁄₁₆in (1.5mm) wide
Silver bell, 1–1 ¼in (2.5–3cm) long (or tiny glass baubles)

Order of work

1. Tie twenty-four thick strands of raffia together at one end (more if they are thinner). Divide the strands into three and plait (braid) evenly. Bind tightly when the plait is 10in (25cm) long, then cut off the remaining raffia. Trim both ends of the plait, then join them neatly with a single strand of raffia, pulling and shaping it to form a flat, circular wreath.
2. Join the cut ends of a 6in (15cm) length of the striped ribbon to form a loop, then fix it over the join in the wreath, to hang it.
3. Bind the remaining striped ribbon round and round the plait, beginning and ending at the top.
4. Bind the wider satin ribbon round the plait in the same way, but in the opposite direction, so that it crosses the striped ribbon.
5. Thread the narrow satin ribbon through the bell (or baubles), and stitch the ends to the top of the wreath so that the decoration hangs.
6. Form the wider ribbon into a 5 ½in (13cm)-wide bow (see page 17 for making mock bows). Bind the middle of the bow with striped ribbon, then stitch it at the top of the wreath, hiding the joins.

Gilded fruits and nuts were another early decoration for the tree, as well as German gingerbread men and spiced honey cakes which, in Scandinavian countries, were usually shaped like little pigs.

For modern versions, wrap crystallized or candied fruit prettily in clear plastic wrap and tie with shiny ribbons. Use model-makers' gold enamel to paint almonds and walnuts, suspending them with fine gold cord or narrow ribbon, perhaps adding a tiny satin bow on top to finish.

The wreath is made of plaited garden raffia but the design could be adapted to ready-made ornaments.

FABERGE BAUBLES

Exquisitely delicate but easy to make, these pretty decorations are inspired by the work of the famous French jewellery designer, Fabergé.

Materials

Large hens' eggs
Sheets of toilet tissue
Prepared wallpaper paste
Deep-toned soft-ply table napkins
 (or face tissues)
Braid, ribbon, lace, beads, tiny
 artificial flower-heads etc, for
 trimming
8in (20cm) satin ribbon, ⅟₁₆in
 (1.5mm) wide, for hangers
One large, and a few smaller beads
 for top decoration for each egg
Sewing thread
Clear adhesive

Order of work

1. Blow the eggs. To do this, make small holes at each end with a darning needle, the one at the rounded end slightly larger than the other. Push the needle inside and stir it around to break the yolk. Then, holding the egg over a basin, blow through the hole at the pointed end until the egg is empty. Wash and dry very thoroughly.
2. To cover each egg, cut one sheet of toilet tissue equally into sixteen pieces and separate the plies.
3. Paste the squares of tissue evenly over the eggs, the edges slightly overlapping (they should form two layers). Place the eggs in a warm oven to hasten drying.
4. Cut more pieces of toilet tissue and apply two more layers to the eggs. Dry, as before.

5. Cut similar-sized pieces of deep-toned tissue and paste three layers over the eggs. Dry thoroughly.

6. Decorate the surface of the egg with braid, ribbon, lace, beads, etc, gluing them neatly into place.

7. Knot the cut ends of the narrow ribbon to form a loop. Push a threaded needle through the larger bead, then through the loop, then back through the bead. Pull the thread through the bead, bringing the ribbon with it.

8. Thread a little circle of smaller beads to fit around the larger bead. Glue the circle to the top of the egg; then glue the bead carrying the loop securely in the centre.

Blown eggshells form the foundation of these baubles — the trimming combines ribbons, braid, lace, beads, sequins, embroidered motifs, tiny flowers — and lots of imagination!

GOLDEN ANGEL

*The Christ-child cherub that originally
adorned the tree gradually evolved into an
angel. This shimmering angel could easily be
adapted to make a fairy.*

Materials

8in (20cm) of gold organdie, 14in
(35cm) wide
8in (20cm) of light-weight gold
taffeta, 36in (90cm) wide
2in (5cm) square of cream-coloured
felt
Clear adhesive
Three pipe cleaners (or chenille
stems), 6½in (16.5cm) long
Flesh-coloured turned paper ball,
1⅜in (3.5cm) diameter
6in (15cm) of cream lace, ⅝in
(15mm) wide
Matching sewing threads
Stiff cardboard
Thin white cardboard
Lurex knitting yarn
6in (15cm) length of tiny pearls
Tiny pins (optional)
Four fluffy white feathers
Dry stick adhesive
Sepia or dark brown pencil or pen

Order of work

1. Cut a piece of organdie 8 x 12in (20 x 30cm) for the underskirt. Join the short edges, right sides facing, to form the centre back seam, then turn a 2in (5cm) hem, making the underskirt 6in (15cm) long. Turn to the right side.
2. Cut a piece of taffeta 8 x 12in (20 x 30cm) for the overskirt. Join the short edges, right sides facing, to form the centre back seam, then turn to the right side. Fold the overskirt in half and baste the raw edges together.
3. Slip the overskirt over the underskirt and pin it so that the folded edge is 1¼in (3cm) above the hem of the underskirt. Join the two together with herringbone stitches working over the raw edge of the overskirt.
4. Cut a piece of taffeta 4 x 12in (10 x 30cm) for the collar. Join the short edges, right sides facing. Turn to the right side and fold the collar, basting the raw edges together.
5. Slip the collar over the two skirts and pin the raw edge of the collar level with the top edge of the underskirt. Turn this whole top edge over to the wrong side and baste, then gather ⅛in (3mm) below the folded edge.
6. To make the arms, cut the hand shape four times from felt. Glue one end of a pipe cleaner between two hands. When dry, trim the hand back to size and shape. Make another arm in the same way with the remaining two felt hands and a pipe cleaner.
7. For sleeves, cut a 6in (15cm) square of gold taffeta. Join two edges, right sides facing. Turn to the right side, fold (as you did for the overskirt) and baste the raw edges together. Gather the raw edges and draw up around the pipe cleaner arm. Then gather ¼in (6mm) above the folded edge and draw up to form a wrist frill around the hand, taking stitches through the top of the hand to hold the frill in place. Make

Work herringbone stitches to attach the overskirt to the underskirt.

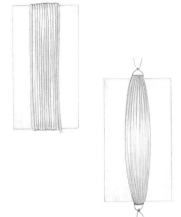

1. Wind yarn evenly around the cardboard.
2. Tie the loops tightly at each edge.

3. Remove from the cardboard and tie the skein loosely at the centre.

4. Glue the tied skeins over the angel's head.

another sleeve in the same way.

8. For the head, bend a pipe cleaner in half and push the bent end into the paper ball. Gather the lace and draw up tightly round the pipe cleaner, just below the ball. Then draw up the dress below the lace.

9. Make a small hole in the organdie underskirt at each side, just above the overskirt. Push the arm pipe cleaners through, to the tops of the sleeves; then push the skirts up in order to bind all the pipe cleaners together with thread, close under the head.

10. For the hair, cut a piece of stiff cardboard 8in (20cm) wide by 5in (12.5cm) deep. Wind the lurex yarn evenly round it 25 times. Then slip an 8in (20cm) length of yarn through the loops at each edge and tie tightly. Slip the yarn off the cardboard and tie the centre loosely. Glue the centre across the top of the ball head, then glue round the sides and knot the ties at the back of the neck.

11. Make a similar skein around a 4½in (11.5cm)-deep piece of cardboard and glue it behind the first

one. Complete the hair with another skein made around a 4in (10cm)-deep piece of cardboard.

12. Cut a 1½in (4cm)-diameter circle of thin cardboard for a halo, and use dry stick adhesive to cover both sides, first with taffeta and then with organdie on top. Trim the fabric level with the edges, then glue pearls around the edges. Glue, or pin, the halo to the back of the head.

13. Glue two feathers together to make each wing, then sew them to the back of the collar so that they spread out behind the angel.

14. Mark the features with brown pencil or pen (refer to the picture). Bend the arms around to the front and glue the hands together.

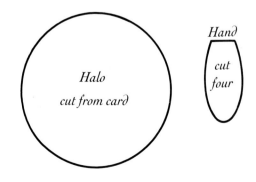

Halo

cut from card

Hand

cut four

CANDY CONES

Little baskets of sweet candies were a favourite Victorian Christmas tree decoration. These cones are quick and easy to make from shimmering foil paper.

Materials

Paper-backed foil gift-wrap paper
Clear adhesive
½yd (40cm) lace, ⅝in (15mm) wide
Sewing thread
¾yd (70cm) grosgrain ribbon, ⅛ – ¼in (3–6mm) wide

Order of work

1. Cut an 8in (20cm)-diameter circle of gift-wrap paper. Fold it in half, right side outside, cutting away a tiny ⅜in (9mm) semi-circle at the centre of the folded edge.
2. Curve the folded circle round to form a cone shape of twice double-thickness paper and glue the overlap.
3. Cut the lace in half. Overlapping the straight edges, flat-stitch the two pieces together to make double-edged lace 1¼in (3cm) wide. Glue the lace around the top edge of the cone.
4. Glue narrow ribbon over the stitched centre of the lace.
5. Glue the cut ends of a 6in (15cm) length of ribbon at each side of the cone to form a handle.
6. Cut the remaining ribbon in half. To make the bows for the handle, mark the centre of each piece, then mark points 1½in (4cm) each side of the centre. Bring the ends round and glue the marked points neatly over the centre. Trim the ribbon ends diagonally for a pretty effect. Glue a bow over each end of the handle.

No Victorian Christmas tree was complete without plenty of pretty, sweet-filled cones.

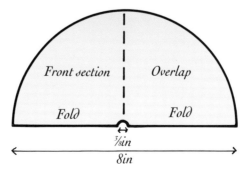

Front section | *Overlap*

Fold | *Fold*

⅜in

8in

Prepare the paper for the cone like this.

BOOTS AND STOCKINGS

Traditional Christmas stockings or Victorian
high-heeled boots — miniature versions of both
with a scented secret.

⤖✹⤙

Materials

STOCKING SACHET
Tracing pattern paper
A piece of plain or printed medium-
 weight cotton-blend fabric,
 4¼ x 6in (11 x 15cm)
Matching sewing thread
Dried lavender or pot-pourri
14in (35cm) of single-face satin
 ribbon ¼in (6mm) wide
4½in (11cm) lengths of braid, ribbon,
 lace, beads etc
Clear adhesive

Tiny stocking sachets make a
delightful, but inexpensive
gift. Use a Christmas printed
cotton fabric if you can.

Order of work

1. Trace the pattern and cut it out.
2. Fold the fabric, right sides together, to measure 4¼ x 3in (11 x 7.5cm). Pin the pattern to the fabric and stitch round it, leaving the top edge of the stocking open.
3. Cut out, using pinking shears, close to the stitching. Cut straight across the top, then remove the pattern. Turn to the right side.
4. Turn under the raw top edges and baste.

X

Stocking sachet

cut from
doubled fabric

5. Fill with lavender or pot-pourri, then oversew the top edges together.

6. Sew the cut ends of an 8in (20cm) length of the satin ribbon at the back corner (x) to form a loop.

7. Glue bands of trimming round the stocking, beginning with the first row slightly overlapping the top edge, and with the join at the back.

8. Make a little bow from the remaining satin ribbon. Glue it to the back of the stocking.

Materials

HIGH BOOT SACHET

Tracing pattern paper
4¼ x 6in (11 x 15cm) of felt
Matching sewing thread
Dried lavender or pot-pourri
8in (20cm) of very narrow ribbon
4⅜in (11cm) lengths of braid, ribbon, lace, beads etc
Four small beads
Clear adhesive

Order of work

1. Trace the pattern and cut it out. Pin the pattern to the felt and cut out the boot shape twice. Oversew the two pieces together all round, leaving the top edge open.

2. Fill the boot with lavender or pot-pourri and oversew the top edge.

3. Sew the ends of the very narrow ribbon to the back corner (x), to form a loop.

4. Glue bands of trimming around the top, slightly overlapping the edges and with the join at the back to form a cuff. Glue a strip of lace down the side of the boot.

5. Sew beads down the side of the boot about ⅜in (9mm) apart.

6. Make a tiny ribbon bow and glue it at the back of the boot.

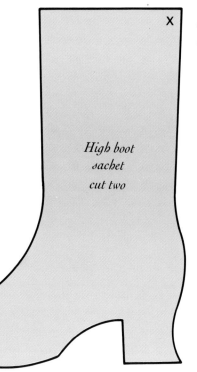

X

*High boot
sachet
cut two*

Choose typically Victorian colours and use tiny beads for the buttons on these little boots.

CHAPTER FIVE

Tidings of comfort and joy ...

CHRISTMAS GREETINGS

THE CHRISTMAS CARD OCCURRED ALMOST BY ACCIDENT. BUT THE ORIGINAL IDEA HAPPENED TO COINCIDE WITH A CUT PRICE POST AND THE DEVELOPMENT OF THE PRINTING INDUSTRY, DUE TO NEW MACHINERY THAT FACILITATED QUALITY COLOUR REPRODUCTION AND INTRICATE PAPER CUTTING. THE GROWTH OF THE PRINTED CHRISTMAS CARD IS A FASCINATING STORY, STARTING WITH THE FIRST CARD IN 1843, DESIGNED BY JOHN CALLCOTT HORSLEY FOR SIR HENRY COLE, TO THE THOUSANDS OF CARDS SENT OUT BY LADIES' CHARITIES TO COMFORT THE POOR AT CHRISTMAS TIME.

The sentimental concept of a 'family Christmas' was nurtured by the timely appearance of the Christmas card. This, in turn, owed its success to another significant development in Britain – the Penny Post.

Until 1840, it was comparatively expensive to send a letter. Only matters of importance were dispatched by mail coach: ordinary folk did not indulge in idle correspondence. But in that year Sir Rowland Hill introduced the Penny Post, making it possible for people to communicate with each other for a reasonable price.

Three years later, in 1843, an imaginative civil servant, Sir Henry Cole, asked a well-known artist, John Callcott Horsley, to design a Christmas greeting card. It depicted a large family group drinking a Christmas toast, and wishing 'A Merry Christmas and a Happy New Year to You'. About a thousand copies of Horsley's card were produced, selling at a shilling. The cards were to be sold in Felix Summerly's Treasure House, an art shop in London's fashionable Bond

Street. However, they were not an instant success; the cards were too expensive for most people – others thought the design trivialised the occasion – and many disapproved of small children drinking alcohol.

By 1870, the custom was slowly becoming firmly established, when the introduction of the halfpenny post in England for cards and unsealed envelopes made the sending of cards to one's friends even more affordable. It was the beginning of a fashion that was slowly to spread throughout the world.

Most of the earlier cards were totally inappropriate for the occasion, showing naked children and winged nymphs enjoying the beauties of sunshine and nature! Slowly the cosy image of Christmas created by Dickens, coupled with the Victorians' enthusiasm for the romantic 'language of flowers', took over. Cards were just as sentimental, but the themes were more suited to the festive season.

Once the combination of cheap cards, cheap postage and artistic designs was established, the Christmas card tradition was all set

ABOVE: Santa and an angel peer through a window at the warm and festive scene inside. As a subject for Christmas cards, angels competed in popularity with Santa Claus: but it is unusual for the two to be shown together.

RIGHT: The first Christmas card, designed in 1843 by John Callcott Horsley for Sir Henry Cole, and sold in Bond Street, London. Priced at one shilling, it was too expensive for most people – and many disapproved of children consuming alcohol. (By kind permission of Hallmark Cards)

A MERRY CHRISTMAS AND A HAPPY NEW YEAR TO YOU

Published at Summerly's Home Treasury Office
12 Old Bond Street, London.   From

to become the vast commercial enterprise that it is today.

The changeover from nymph-like children with no clothes on, to the traditional subjects that we now associate with Christmas, took time. But eventually Victorian cards accompanied their greeting with snow scenes, holly, ivy and mistletoe, bells, Christmas roses, ice-skating and stage coaches. There were angels and cherubs in abundance, but specific religious themes did not appear. The cards were often embellished with decorative scraps, lace, gold and silver highlights and glitter. The messages were always effusive and over-sentimental.

In England, the red-breasted robin was especially popular, perhaps because the bird provides a welcome flash of colour in the winter, when so many other birds have migrated. In pagan mythology he symbolized life-giving fire during the winter solstice. His red breast is attributed to several causes: some believe that he was scorched by flames – either attempting to rescue sinners from hell, or fanning the embers of a dying fire to help Mary keep the baby Jesus warm. Others say that his feathers were smeared with Christ's blood as the robin tried to ease his pain on the cross, either by removing the thorns pricking his head, or by pulling out a nail. Whatever story you prefer, the robin is always seen as a fearless, friendly, self-sacrificing bird.

Flowers were another popular, if unseasonal, subject. Often the card carried a message in the 'language of flowers', which gave every bloom a special meaning. Evergreens, in particular, appeared regularly – since they represented everlasting friendship. Little girls with long blonde curls were still very much in evidence, but they were now fully

LEFT: Kate Greenaway was an outstandingly prolific artist in the latter half of the nineteenth century. Her books and charming illustrations of young people were popular with Victorians of all ages. This demure little girl, with her big hat and cosy muff, is typical of her work.

dressed in fur-trimmed outfits and leggings, smiling shyly behind a bunch of mistletoe or an outsize muff, as they wished you a Merry Christmas and a Happy New Year.

Charitably-minded English ladies saw the Christmas card as a rather touching way to reach the needy and underprivileged. The Christmas Card Mission cheered many lonely, poor people in hospitals, work-houses, prisons and similar institutions all over Britain. The card was always accompanied by a friendly letter carrying warm wishes and a few sympathetic words of encouragement.

The ladies who sent the first cards were so surprised and gratified to discover how much the gesture was appreciated, that they set out to reach everyone who might need a few words of comfort at Christmas-time. As a result, the Mission grew so fast that in only a few years it was sending out thousands of cards every December. These were delivered so that the recipient awoke to find the envelope beside his or her pillow on Christmas morning.

ABOVE: Robins in the snow were a favourite subject for Christmas cards – as they are now – but in the United States, robins tend to migrate south in winter and the red poinsettia flower is more often featured on American greeting cards.

CHILDREN IN CROSS STITCH

*Three young Victorians are ready for
Christmas. Have fun changing the colour
schemes to give them different outfits.*

Materials

A piece of cream Aida fabric 5 x 4¾in
(12.5 x 12cm) with sixteen blocks
of threads to 1in (2.5cm) for each
card
Stranded embroidery cottons (floss)
in the colours on the charts and
gold thread
Blank greeting cards with a 4 x 3⅛in
(10 x 8cm) oval window
Clear adhesive
Gold ricrac braid

Order of work

1. Work the design from the charts in
cross stitch, following the colour key.
Use two strands of embroidery
cotton throughout. Work the mouths
in Rose 335/38. Where gold thread is
used, work with three strands. Work
the noses and outline the boy's face in
light brown backstitch.
2. Outline the figures and pick out
the design in backstitch using a single
strand of black.
3. Trim the fabric to fit inside the
card, then mount it behind the
window. Glue ricrac braid around the
window with a small bow at the top.

Work the designs from the
charts. Each square
represents one cross stitch.

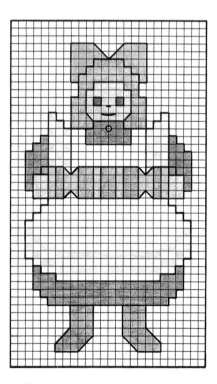
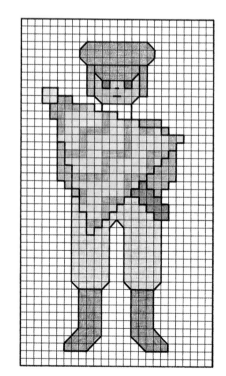
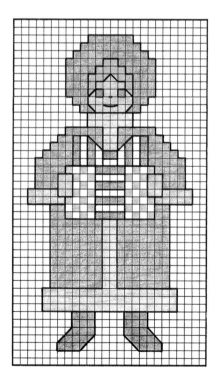

DMC	ANCHOR	DMC	ANCHOR
336 Dark blue	133	415 Mid-grey	398
794 Mid-blue	130	970 Orange	324
775 Pale blue	128	470 Mid-olive	265
754 Flesh	6	937 Deep olive	267
310 Black	403	869 Mid-brown	375
700 Emerald	229	3045 Camel	373
321 Scarlet	46	White	01
938 Dark brown	381	Fil or Clair (gold)	Kreinik (gold)
552 Purple	93		

A modern presentation of the most popular subject for Victorian greetings. The cards could also be framed to make small pictures.

$\mathcal{S}$ILHOUETTE COLLAGE

Silhouettes were popular in the nineteenth century. This design makes three different greeting cards.

⟩⟨✳⟩⟨

Materials

Tissue or tracing paper
Dry stick adhesive
Black paper
Yellow and cream paper
Red, white and cream window
    greeting cards
Small paper doily
Small flower motif
20in (50cm) narrow lace edging
20in (50cm) gold ribbon, ⅛in (3mm)
    wide
Clear adhesive

RIGHT: Three different interpretations of the same design. Purchased mounts give hand-made cards a very professional finish.

Order of work

1. Trace the design onto good quality white tissue paper or tracing pattern

Trace this outline

The small girl and her doll was inspired by a sketch made by Queen Victoria of her eldest daughter Vicky, in 1846.

paper. Trace the outline through to the other side of the tissue paper. Then, using dry stick adhesive, glue the tracing to the back of medium-weight black paper. Cut very carefully around the tracing. Glue it into position on the card mount.

To decorate the mounts

2. RED CARD. Mount the cut out silhouette on a piece of yellow paper then set it behind the window. Edge the oval with sections cut from the outer edges of a small paper doily gluing them in place with dry stick adhesive. Finish by gluing on a trimming of small red and green flowers.

3. WHITE CARD. Mount the silhouette on cream paper. Cut lace edging to shape for the rectangular card, making sure the corners are aligned accurately. Make four mock bows from 2¾in (7cm) lengths of gold ribbon and glue these to the corners. (Refer to page 17 for making mock bows.)

4. CREAM CARD. Mount the silhouette on yellow paper then set it behind the window. Make a 2in (5cm)-wide mock bow from a 3¼in (8cm) length of gold ribbon. Make a gold ribbon rose and glue it to the centre of the bow. Glue to the card. (Refer to page 19 for making ribbon roses.)

CHAPTER SIX

Bless all the dear children ...

THE CHILDREN'S CHRISTMAS

In the past, Christmas had been a convivial occasion for adults to indulge in abandoned revelry and feasting. But in the nineteenth century everything changed, and children became the focus of the festivities. Encouraged by pictures of the Queen and her husband celebrating with their large family, Christmas became a special time for children. The arrival of Santa Claus, first in America, then soon afterwards in England, made Christmas the children's own festival.

Undoubtedly, children in earlier centuries enjoyed the Yule log festivities. Nevertheless, the pre-Victorian English Christmas was very much an adult affair. Children were merely bystanders, laughing at the antics of the Lord of Misrule (master of Christmas revelries in the fifteenth and sixteenth centuries), while not understanding his lewd jokes, and entertained by the mummers' plays (mime shows) and the dancing, joining in the bawdy songs and savouring the spicy food. But there were no presents, no stockings and no fireside family reunions. And in the many homes which disapproved of the unruly behaviour of the Lord of Misrule and his followers, Christmas was just like any other day.

Then suddenly, after centuries of riotous communal revelry, the mid-nineteenth century saw the outside activities replaced by a much quieter celebration centred on the home with

ABOVE: The red-robed Father Christmas figure that we know today was imagined and developed by various American artists, notably Thomas Nast and Thomas Beale. They were most probably inspired by the enormously popular poem, 'The Night Before Christmas' by Clement Clarke Moore, a New York professor.

RIGHT: A touching picture of peaceful tranquility that demonstrates how, by the end of the century, Christmas had become a sentimental time, focused on the children. Santa rummages through his sack to find suitable toys to fill the cherubs' waiting stockings.

the focus on the children. Christmas became *their* special time. The pretty candlelit tree hung with sparkling decorations and tiny toys, gingerbread and sweets. Dolls and model soldiers, picture books, performing monkeys, skittles, humming tops, money-boxes, tin trumpets and drums filled the toyshops, waiting to find comfortable homes with good little girls and boys. Sleighbells rang and the skaters were out on the frozen ponds, hands tucked into fur muffs and ears hidden deep within the brims of velvet bonnets and warm caps. The idealized concept of the Victorian Christmas is complete.

But all was not sweetness and light. In the slums of Victorian Britain's industrial towns and cities, there was appalling poverty. And, as always, it was the children who suffered most. The new 'family' Christmas was intended to expose their misery – if only for one day in the year.

A charming scene that epitomizes the Victorian family Christmas. Grand-parents, whose generation would have known a very different kind of childhood Christmas, with no tree or presents, share the children's delight in their new toys.

Parties were organized in schools and halls: poor children gazed in wonder at the Christmas tree – often the gift of a member of the Royal Family – and clutched the toy and bag of sweet candies which they were given to take home. In this way, the new Victorian-style Christmas reached the poor, too: and it was the children who were singled out for extra-special treatment.

For children, the two momentous events of the Victorian era were the invention of the Christmas cracker in 1840, and the arrival of Santa Claus in the 1860s.

The American version of Santa Claus was based on the legendary Siner Klaas – Saint Nicholas – who arrived in America with the seventeenth-century Dutch settlers, and was later known as Santiclaus.

Saint Nicholas was a fourth-century Turkish bishop and the patron saint of children – and Russia, scholars, sailors, pawnbrokers,

parish clerks, virgins and thieves – a very popular patron saint! In Holland, he came down the chimney to fill the stockings of good children with presents – or to leave a birch rod for the bad ones. This kind of logic appealed to the Victorians, who had very definite theories about discipline and the meting out of justice in the nursery. Charles Dickens' *A Christmas Carol* had been successful in America, too, and St Nicholas's principle of rewarding the good and punishing the wicked exemplified the new nineteenth-century morality that the book conveyed.

The Christmas stocking was another product of the Santa Claus legend, and this soon caught on too. The original Saint Nicholas was a generous and charitable man. One day he threw a bag of coins through a poor man's window. A pair of his daughter's stockings was hanging in front of the fire to dry and, by chance, the gold fell into one of them. Since then, children have hung up their stockings on Christmas Eve, with a letter telling Santa what they would like him to bring them when he comes down the chimney – having left his sleigh and reindeer on the roof.

It was essential for the stocking to contain an apple and an orange, representing health and good living respectively, and a bright new penny for prosperity. A lump of coal and some salt was often added, for warmth and good fortune. For poor children, this was often all. But better-off parents had no difficulty finding all manner of toys and trinkets with which to fill the stocking.

Victorian toyshops were an Aladdin's cave of wonderful things to tempt children of all ages. Many came from Prince Albert's own

The children of well-to-do families could hope to receive some very impressive and imaginative presents. Every branch of the toymaking industry flourished and expanded enormously, and toyshops were a wonderland of temptation for children and indulgent parents alike.

country, for Germany was a land of toymakers, producing not only beautifully carved wooden toys but also mechanical toys and automata – clockwork vehicles, performing clowns and musical boxes – and also the kind of beautifully dressed dolls that every little girl dreamed about. However, even those lucky enough to have their wish fulfilled, were often only allowed to play with such expensive dolls on Sunday afternoons. Those with wax faces were particularly realistic and beautiful, but many of these met with disaster when their caring owner sat them too close to the fire.

Boys too were spoilt for choice. Model soldiers, Noah's Arks, hobby-horses, jumping-Jack puppets, trains, cannons, marbles, yo-yos, skipping ropes, fishing games and jigsaw puzzles were just some of the toyshop temptations. Board games were very popular with children of all ages, and new ones based on topical themes were constantly appearing on the market.

Colour printing was a fast-

developing industry, producing a variety of fascinating pastimes for children. Printed sheets, with a drawing of a doll and a series of interchangeable outfits for the child to cut out, were enormously popular. An extension of the paper doll was the toy theatre, with printed sheets providing the stage and curtains and all the characters for well-known plays and pantomimes, together with a change of scenery for each act.

But now a knocking at the door was heard and such a rush...just in time to greet the father, who came home attended by a man laden with Christmas toys and presents. Then the shouting and the struggling ... to dive into his pockets, despoil him of brown-paper parcels....The shouts of wonder and delight with which the development of every package was received! The terrible announcement that the baby had been taken in the act of putting a doll's frying pan into his mouth, and was more than suspected of having swallowed a fictitious turkey, glued on a wooden platter! The immense relief of finding this a false alarm! The joy, and gratitude, and ecstasy! They are all indescribably alike. It is enough that, by degrees, the children and their emotions got out of the parlour, and, by one stair at a time, up to the top of the house, where they went to bed, and so subsided.

From *A Christmas Carol* by Charles Dickens.

TOP: Just as it still does today, the Christmas stocking held a wonderful fascination for children. This amusing card imagines every child's dream: the thrill of trying to guess the contents of a giant stocking packed with toys.

ABOVE: Dolls were always beautifully dressed, with wax or porcelain heads. And models of soldiers on horseback were often too delicate for the rough and tumble of the nursery. Musical instruments were specially popular, and so was a Noah's Ark full of animals – in pairs, of course!

PARLOUR GAMES AND ENTERTAINMENT

Scrooge's niece was not one of the blindman's-buff party, but was made comfortable with a large chair and a footstool, in a snug corner where the Ghost and Scrooge were close behind her. But she joined in the forfeits, and loved her love to admiration with all the letters of the alphabet. Likewise at the game of How, When and Where, she was very great, and, to the secret joy of Scrooge's nephew, beat her sisters hollow: though they were sharp girls too, as Topper could have told you.

From *A Christmas Carol* by Charles Dickens

*M*ost of the very old games traditionally played at Christmas centred around some form of strong drink. On Christmas Eve it was Snap dragon. The bottom of a wide bowl was covered with raisins; brandy was poured over, and then lit. The lights were extinguished and everyone tried to grab the raisins without burning their fingers in the flames.

Victorian parlour games were less adventurous than the things young people got up to in the Middle Ages, but still provided an opportunity for plenty of flirting and fondling – if the young lady permitted – and often she did. If the new Victorian morality was eased just a little, at least it was all happening in the home, and no doubt mama kept a firm eye on what was going on.

Hide-and-seek was a great favourite, as was Blindman's buff, which gave the blindfolded young man the chance to pinch the arm, and even squeeze the waist, of every willing female. The Victorians loved to act, and charades were very popular, while 'Forfeits' provided much hilarious, but harmless, fun: these ranged from singing a song or pretending to be a nesting bird to kissing a lady through the back of a chair.

When the younger ones had exhausted themselves chasing each other around the house – hunting the slipper or the thimble – there were plenty of table games to provide less energetic amusement. Spillikins (a game played with sticks) and Pope Joan, an exciting card game, were two particular favourites, but there was the 'Meteor Ball mosaic game' for making patterns with coloured balls; 'Fishponds', a parlour game for four persons, which entailed using a short rod and line to pick up objects representing fish; 'Gypsy', a fortune-telling game; and many 'question-and-answer' games, the questions usually based on the Bible, history or

'Here comes a chopper to chop off your head . . .'
With hearts thumping, the children rush through the arch to escape the final moment of 'Oranges and Lemons'.
The centuries-old rhyming game is based on the bells of the churches in the City of London.

geography – which might have been forerunners of today's 'Trivial Pursuit'.

Card games were played with enthusiasm, and both American and British manufacturers launched endless new versions. 'Happy Families' was a great favourite, and one outstandingly popular American card game involved a lighthearted character called Dr Busby.

At Windsor, Queen Victoria sang duets with her husband Prince Albert, and they both enjoyed playing spillikins and puzzling over alphabet games. Everyone at the royal court became very excited when a new round game called *main jaune* was introduced, which they all agreed they preferred to *mouche*, a previous favourite. Gambling was quite acceptable when they played *vingt-et-un* or Pope Joan, though the stakes were low, and threepence was considered a sizeable win. The Royal children acted charades and played forfeits, to the amusement of the adults. There were balls, too, where guests danced minuets, quadrilles, reels, Scottish jigs and country dances.

In country districts, bands of mummers – travelling actors – still performed their traditional plays at Christmas time, just as they had in the medieval festivities around the Yule log. 'George and the Dragon' was the most popular story, telling how St George fought off not only the dragon, but also a Turkish knight. The ritual story represented the triumph of life over death, and the script had been handed down from one generation to the next for almost a thousand years. The actors blackened their faces or wore animal masks, and dressed in ragged costumes made from strips of paper. Mummers provided Christmas entertainment in many American states, too. But their popularity declined towards the end of the century, after the police had to break up unruly audiences in Baltimore.

Blindman's buff was a special favourite – with both young and old. Those who were caught had to pay a forfeit. The tasks that were demanded were often quite outrageous, and the cause of even more merriment.

VICKY – THE SUFFOLK PUFF DOLL

A demure little doll to enchant young and old alike. She would be equally at home in a little girl's nursery or on a not-so-little girl's dressing table.

※

Materials

Medium-weight, cotton-blend floral print dress fabric, 36 x 14in (90 x 35cm) wide

Matching, and black, sewing threads

Medium-weight, cotton-blend white fabric, 36 x 14in (90 x 35cm) wide

Tracing pattern paper

Piece of cream-coloured felt, 4¾ x 8in (12 x 20cm)

Washable polyester toy filling

Piece of black felt, 3 x 4in (7.5 x 10cm)

Scrap of stiff cardboard

1½yd (1.4m) of narrow, round elastic

24in (60cm) of broderie anglaise (eyelet embroidery), 1in (2.5cm) wide

36in (90cm) of black lace, ⅜in (9mm) wide

Stranded embroidery wool (or fine knitting yarn)

Brown domed sequins, about 3/16in (5mm) diameter

Pink-red stranded embroidery cotton (floss)

Heavyweight sew-in interfacing

Fusible interfacing

Clear adhesive

18in (45cm) of narrow braid

6in (15cm) of satin ribbon, ¼in (6mm) wide

Note: Seam allowances: Oversew the edges of felt to join. Take ¼in (6mm) seams when stitching fabric.

Order of work

1. TO MAKE A PUFF. Draw a circle with compasses to the required size directly onto the wrong side of the fabric. Fold it into four, matching the cut edges carefully. Then snip off just the very tip of the folded corner to make a tiny hole, before opening up the circle again. Gather all round with evenly-spaced running stitches, close to the raw edges. With the wrong side of the fabric inside, pull the thread ends up to draw up the edges of the circle. Flatten the puff with the raw edges in the middle. Fasten off the thread ends.

2. Make up the following puffs, cutting the fabric circles to the size indicated:

IN FLORAL FABRIC:

Six circles: 4in (10cm) diameter (A)

Eight circles: 3in (7.5cm) diameter (B)

Twelve circles: 2¼in (6cm) diameter (C)

IN WHITE FABRIC:

Two circles: 5½in (13cm) diameter (D)

One circle: 4¾in (12cm) diameter (E)

One circle: 4in (10cm) diameter (F)

Twenty-four circles: 3in (7.5cm) diameter (G)

3. HEAD. Trace the pattern pieces and cut out. Cut one face and three back head pieces from cream felt. Join two back head pieces between A–B. Join the third piece in the same way, but leave open between the notches. Join the head to each side of the face,

Made from round 'puffs' of fabric (a traditional old English country craft), Vicky's body needs no stuffing. Choose a tiny floral print for her dress.

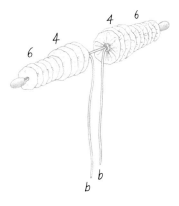

1. Measure and mark the elastic, thread on the sleeve puffs, sew on the hands.

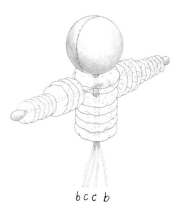

2. Sew the centre of the body elastic underneath the head. Thread all four elastics down through the upper body puffs.

3. Sew elastic to the feet and thread on the pantalette puffs.

matching points A–B. Turn to the right side and stuff very firmly, then close the seam.

4. HANDS. Cut four hands from cream felt. For each hand, oversew two pieces together all round, leaving the straight edge open. Turn to the right side and stuff. Gather around the top edge and draw up (*not* too tightly), then oversew the gathered edges.

5. FEET. Cut two shoes and two soles from black felt. For each foot, join the front of the shoe between C–D. Then fit the lower edge round the sole, matching the notches (E) and with the seam at centre front and back. Oversew together. Turn to the right side. Cut the sole again, slightly smaller, in cardboard. Fit inside the shoe, then stuff. Gather round the top edge and partially draw up, then oversew the edges together.

6. ASSEMBLY. Cut an 18in (45cm) length of round elastic; mark the centre with a pin. Measure 2¾in (7cm) each side of the pin (a). Fold the elastic and push the loops through the centre of four B floral puffs, and then six C puffs. Sew a hand to the elastic, but sew *through the loop*, so that the hand can be moved along the elastic.

7. Sew the centre of an 8in (20cm) length of elastic underneath the head. Push the cut ends (c) through two A floral puffs. Then slip the arms elastic

between the two head elastics and take all four ends (b) and (c) down through the remaining four A floral puffs, and then through the single white F puff.

8. Sew the centre of a 12in (30cm) length of elastic to the top of a shoe. Then thread the cut ends (d) through twelve white G puffs. Make another leg in the same way.

9. Now push all four ends (d) through the two white D puffs and then the white E puff. Space the puffs out evenly along the elastic; then, one at a time, knot all the ends together: (b and d, b and d, c and d, c and d). Sew each knot to prevent it slipping, then trim off the ends.

10. PETTICOAT. Cut a piece of white fabric 4⅜in (11cm) deep x 14in (35cm) wide. Join the short edges to form the centre back seam. Trim the bottom edge with broderie anglaise (eyelet embroidery) to overlap the raw edge by ½in (1cm). Gather the top edge, then fit the petticoat on the doll and draw up the gathers tightly round the elastic beneath the lowest floral puff. Secure the thread ends.

11. SKIRT. Cut a piece of floral fabric 5½in (13cm) x 16in (40cm) wide. Join the short edges to form the centre back seam. Turn up and stitch a ½in (1cm) hem and trim the skirt with black lace just above the lower edge. Gather the top edge and fit it on the doll, over the petticoat.

12. Take a thread up through the top of the skirt and through the body puffs, close to the centre front – then back again – catching them down.

13. HAIR. Separate three 30in (75cm) strands of wool, then put them together again and fold the bunch into four. Stitch the middle of the bunch to the centre of the forehead using matching thread, then take the ends smoothly down over each side of the face and around to the back. Sew in place securely.

14. Prepare another three strands in the same way and stitch them close behind the first ones, taking them around to the back and finishing off as before. Continue until the head is almost covered. When the uncovered area is quite small, fold the wool into six – and finally, into eight.

15. FACE. Pin the eye sequins to the face to determine their position. When you are satisfied, sew them into place with black thread. Then, using the thread doubled, work short straight stitches for the eyebrows and nose. Embroider a V-shape with three strands of pink-red embroidery cotton (floss) for the mouth.

16. COLLAR AND CUFFS. Gather an 8in (20cm) length of lace and draw it up to fit around the neck, joining the ends at the back. Gather two 6in (15cm) lengths of lace to fit around the doll's wrists.

17. BONNET. Cut the bonnet brim and back from heavyweight interfacing. Using fusible interfacing, bond floral fabric to both sides, folding it over the straight edges and trimming the cut edges neatly. Place the straight edge of the brim to the bonnet back, matching points F and the notch, and oversew together. Glue braid over the stitches and around the front edge of the brim.

18. FRILL. Gather an 8in (20cm) length of broderie anglaise (eyelet embroidery). Pin it evenly over the top of the head and draw up. Fit the bonnet on top and adjust the gathers if necessary. Remove the bonnet and sew the frill into place.

19. Make a tiny bow near the centre of the ribbon and sew the ends to the sides of the head, so that the bow is under the chin. Finally, sew the bonnet into place.

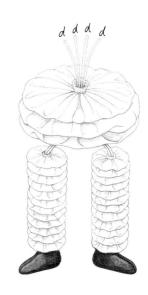

4. Thread all four leg elastics through the lower body puffs.

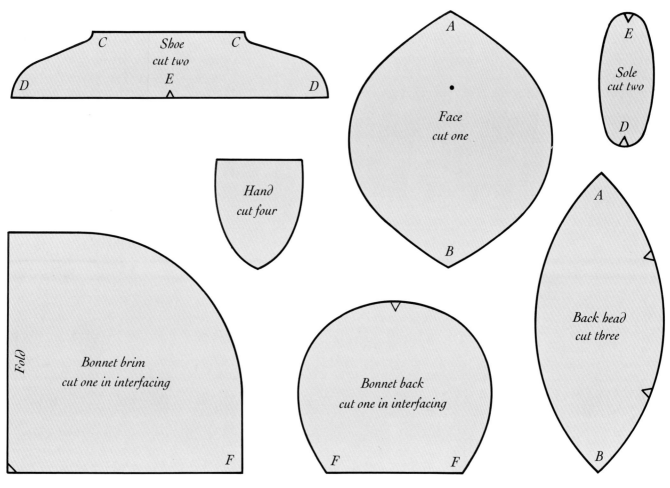

TOY SOLDIER SKITTLES

*A group of smartly uniformed soldiers –
proudly playing their instruments. The
skittles made mainly from paper.*

❧❋❧

Materials

Three sheets of medium-weight
white paper 8¼ x 11½in
(21 x 29cm)
Black felt-tipped pen
Clear adhesive
8in (20cm) length of blue ribbon,
¼in (6mm) wide
Sheets of good quality waste paper
(magazines, etc)
6in (15cm) square of red felt
Tracing pattern paper
2⅜ x 3in (6 x 7.5cm) white felt
4⅜in (11cm) length of gold braid
Two tiny red beads
Red and white sewing threads
4⅜ x 6in (11 x 15cm) piece of black
felt
Pale pink paper
Black paper
Brown paper
Gold gift-tie, ¼in (6mm) wide
(optional)
6in (15cm) length of black ribbon,
¼in (6mm) wide
Assorted gold sequins
8in (20cm) length of white ribbon,
¼in (6mm) wide
30in (75cm) length of white ribbon,
1⁄16in (1.5mm) wide
Thin cardboard
Coloured paper; thin cord; tooth
picks; thin skewer; bead

Order of work

1. Lay a sheet of white paper
widthways and, from the left, mark
off 5in (12.5cm). Mark the right-
hand area 'overlap'. On the left-hand
area, pencil a line from top to bottom.
Make a short horizontal line across,
1⅜in (3.5cm) from the top edge (the
hair and helmet position). Measure
and mark, in black pen, a central,
vertical line 2¾in (7cm) up from the
bottom edge for the legs.

2. Mark, in pencil, vertical lines 1¼in
(3cm) away to each side. Cut and
glue 4¼in (11cm) lengths of blue
ribbon for the trousers stripe.

3. Beginning at the right-hand edge,
roll up into a tube 1⅝in (4cm) in
diameter, matching the long edges,
and glue the overlap. Roll up the
other two sheets of white paper and
fit them inside the tube, allowing
them to open out to fit snugly against
the sides. Fill up the inside with
several more sheets of waste paper,
cut to size.

4. JACKET. Cut a piece of red felt
5½in wide by 2¾in deep (14 x 7cm).
Mark the arm positions 1⅜in (3.5cm)
in from the sides and ⅜in (9mm)
down from the top edge.

5. Trace the arm pattern onto thin
cardboard twice and cut out. Glue
red felt to both sides of the cardboard
arms up to the broken line. Then
cover the gloved hands, to the broken
line, with white felt. Glue 1¼in (3cm)

of gold braid around the top edge of the gloves.

6. Sew the arms to each side of the jacket. Pass the needle through the arm then through a red bead, then into the jacket at the placement mark. Work back and forth several times so that the arm is secure and moves easily.

7. HELMET. Using the pattern, cut the helmet top from cardboard, and glue it to black felt. Cut V-shaped notches on the edges to form tiny tabs (see pattern). Place the helmet top on the top of the tube and glue the tabs down to hold it in place. Cut a piece of black felt 5½in wide by 1½in deep (14 x 3.7cm) for the helmet.

8. FACE. Cut the face from pink paper. Cut the helmet peak in black paper. Glue the peak to the face (marked on the pattern with a

A set of model soldiers was every boy's ambition – and skittles was another favourite activity to be found in all the toy shops.

broken line) then mark the features in black.

9. Glue the face to the tube, the top edge level with the marked horizontal line. Glue a 1¼in (3cm)-deep strip of brown paper round the tube for hair, cutting it so that it overlaps the face as indicated by the vertical broken lines on the pattern.

10. Glue the helmet strip around the tube, overlapping the face as indicated by the broken line on the pattern. Overlap the edges at the back.

11. Glue the jacket around the tube, overlapping the face as indicated by the broken line on the pattern. Overlap the edges at the back. Glue gold gift-tie around the jacket for a collar. Glue black ribbon around for a belt. Glue on the sequin buttons. Arrange the wide, white ribbon over the shoulder and across the back and chest, gluing it together at the side, following the picture.

12. Glue gift-tie around the bottom of the helmet.

13. Cut ten 2¾in (7cm) lengths of very narrow white ribbon and bind together tightly at the centre, then fold in half and bind tightly again, close to the fold. Glue to the helmet for a cockade. Trim the cut ends neatly. Glue narrow braid around the face.

14. FEET. Cut a ¾in (2cm)-diameter circle of black felt in half for feet. Glue them to the base of the figure at each side of the vertical legs line.

15. INSTRUMENTS. Small, musical tree decorations can be purchased for instruments.

TO MAKE A DRUM. Cut several 1 x 12in (2.5 x 30cm) lengths of paper. Roll one up from a short end and glue to form a ring about 2in (5cm) in diameter. Roll up the remaining strips and fit them inside, allowing them to open up against the outer ring. Cut two 2⅜in (6cm)-diameter circles of thin white cardboard and glue one to each side of the paper ring, keeping them level. Cut a 1⅜ x 8in (3.5 x 20cm) strip of coloured paper and glue it around the outside of the drum. Trim with gift-tie ribbon and fix thin cord through the top edges of the drum to hang round the soldier's neck. Glue toothpicks to the hands for drumsticks. Glue a large bead to the tip of a 5½in (14cm)-long thin wooden skewer for a baton.

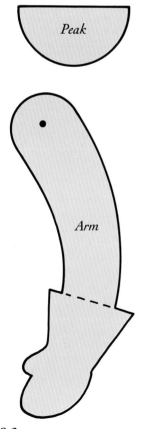

Peak

Arm

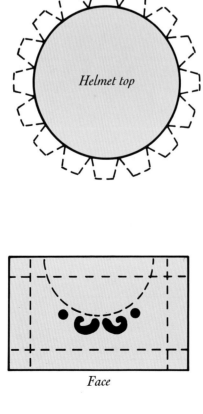

Helmet top

Face

Trace these pattern pieces

$\mathscr{B}$ERIBBONED
CHRISTMAS STOCKING

*Here is an inexpensive way to make the most
spectacular stockings that Santa is likely to
fill! Ribbon, lace and braid are combined for the
lavish decoration.*

Materials

Graph pattern paper
Two pieces of medium-weight, plain
  or printed, cotton-blend fabric,
  18 x 10in (45 x 25cm)
Assorted lengths and widths of
  ribbon, lace, braid etc
Matching sewing threads

Order of work

1. Draw the pattern on graph paper, extending the leg lines to 14in (35cm). Cut out. Cut the stocking twice in fabric.
2. Arrange the trimmings on one piece of stocking. Baste, then machine-stitch in place.
3. Taking a ¼in (6mm) seam allowance, join the two stocking pieces, right sides facing, stitching all round but leaving the straight top edge open. Trim and clip into the seams to ease the curves. Turn to the right side. Press.
4. Turn the top edge under and sew a hem. Then trim the top of the stocking.
5. Make four mock bows to trim the front. (Refer to page 17 for making mock bows.)
6. Form a 12in (30cm) length of ribbon into a loop and sew it inside the top back of the stocking.

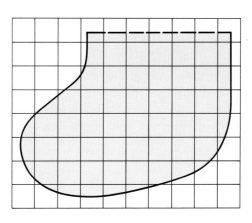

Scale: 1 sq = 1in (2.5cm)

If the stocking is to be lined, cut the pattern twice again from plain fabric. Stitch, right sides facing, slip into the finished stocking and oversew the top edges together.

CHAPTER SEVEN

Bearing gifts, we travel afar ...

A TIME FOR GIVING

Christmas presents were not exchanged until the latter part of the century, when Americans invented the scarlet-clad figure of Santa Claus. Poor children were the first to benefit from Santa's bulging sack, but soon everyone was giving and receiving gifts. Handiwork skills were put to good use making attractive presents for family and friends. The Victorians quite rightly believed that hand-made gifts were special and showed their love and affection. They excelled at making pretty things with a personal touch.

Much they saw, and far they went, and many homes they visited, but always with a happy end. The Spirit stood beside sick-beds, and they were cheerful; on foreign lands, and they were close at home; by struggling men, and they were patient in their greatest hope; by poverty, and it was rich. In almshouse, hospital, and gaol, in misery's every refuge, where vain man in his little brief authority had not made fast the door, and barred the Spirit out, he left his blessing and taught Scrooge his precepts.

From *A Christmas Carol* by Charles Dickens

The European Santa was usually depicted on foot while the American one travelled through the sky on a sleigh from the North pole. This idea might have been influenced by the legend of the Norse god, Odin, who distributed presents to children from his night sky chariot.

Gifts were always exchanged at the Roman festivals of Saturnalia and Kalends – while in Northern Europe, where the feast of Yule was observed, the Norse god Odin was known as the Gift-Bringer. But the giving of gifts at Christmas was frowned upon by the early Christian church because of its connections with these pagan winter solstice celebrations. Instead, until the last quarter of the nineteenth century, it was customary for adults to give each other presents at New Year and Twelfth Night. It was not until Christmas finally took over in importance as a festival that it became general to exchange presents on Christmas Day – and for children to be included. And, even when the New Year had ceased to be celebrated, many people still exchanged gifts on that day.

Christmas as we know it was 'invented' to awaken a social conscience among the well-to-do Victorians. It was a time to remember the poor: to do all one could to bring the new spirit of Christmas into their lives to relieve their poverty and suffering.

More and more it was impressed upon English Victorian ladies of the leisured classes that it was their duty to devote time to work for charity, and the majority took this task very seriously. They organized Christmas benevolent funds in an efficient and businesslike manner, encouraging others to give generously. They undoubtedly did much to brighten the lives of many poor people, especially the children.

Food was always at the top of the list, but warm clothing came a close second. Hand-knitted mittens and woolly mufflers, socks and stockings were distributed by the charitable ladies, who arranged sewing groups and working parties of friends to make the garments. Gifts of sweet candies, fruit, tea, tobacco and snuff were added, and thus many poor people enjoyed their happiest day of the year. Stout boots were often handed out to barefoot children although these were not always so popular, as they were *so* stout that they were instantly recognizable as 'charity boots'.

It was only sensible that the gifts should be of a practical nature. But when Santa Claus – the American version of Saint Nicholas – arrived in England, he set the scene for something even more exciting for children who had probably never owned a toy in their lives.

Considerable funds were raised by Victorian women – who then took a delight in dressing up to play the part of Santa Claus. In this guise they toured the slums, visiting homes to distribute presents to destitute families, delving down into Santa's sack to find a toy for each child.

This kind of caring had long been an established tradition in English country areas, where a good landlord, or the village squire, would send his tenants their Christmas dinner. And his womenfolk would visit the families in their cottages, taking gifts of food and clothing.

Following the example of Queen Victoria and her family, sweet candies and small gifts from the tree were distributed to the children and servants on Christmas Day. This revived a centuries-old custom that had all but died out in the seventeenth century. But serious present-giving did not begin to take place until the 1870s, when it was introduced by Santa Claus – drawn through the sky by reindeer, with a sackload of presents in his sleigh. Then middle-class children began hanging up their stockings, and looking forward to their presents on Christmas Day.

Adults, of course, were not to be left out. Clothing, jewellery, slippers and books were popular presents. But the Victorians' love of knick-knacks, coupled with their frantic enthusiasm for crafts, meant that there was no shortage of hand-made gifts – ranging from embroidered pen-wipers to rustic picture frames made from twigs!

For children, the choice was equally eclectic. For little ones, a rocking horse, a mechanical clockwork mouse, an india-rubber dog or a Berlin wool-embroidered elephant. Older children would have enjoyed a game of shuttlecock (badminton), a toy piano or a set of gardening tools.

Small boys must have loved the juvenile tool chest, the mechanical steamboat and schooner in full sail and the brass cannon.

It took time for the Victorians to catch on to the idea of Christmas presents. But when they did – they left us a legacy which has grown into such a massive commercial event that it keeps the shops busy throughout the whole of the winter solstice!

A moving example of the true spirit of the Victorian Christmas. Toys taken down from the tree are distributed to children at a foundling hospital in 1881.

OLDING

PHOTOGRAPH FRAME

This very attractive small double frame is free-standing, and can easily be scaled-up to make a larger portrait-sized frame, if you wish.

Materials

Tracing pattern paper
Medium-weight cardboard
Stiff cardboard
6 x 28in (15 x 70cm) of firmly-woven, medium-weight printed cotton-blend fabric
Dry stick adhesive
Matching sewing thread
Clear adhesive
24in (60cm) of Russian braid (to tone with the fabric)

Order of work

1. Trace the frame pattern very carefully, then transfer twice onto the medium-weight cardboard. Cut out, cutting away the oval window.
2. Trace the outline of the frame twice more onto the same, medium-weight cardboard, omitting the oval. Cut out.
3. Trace the outline of the frame onto the stiff cardboard. Cut out.
4. Cut four 5¼ x 4in (13 x 10cm) pieces of fabric, one piece 5¼ x 8in (13 x 20cm) and one piece 4 x 1in (10 x 2.5cm).
5. Cover the surface of one of the cardboard frame with window pieces with stick adhesive, then place it centrally on the wrong side of a smaller piece of fabric. Mitre the corners, and cut V-shaped notches across the top edge to form tabs. Then fold the surplus fabric neatly over and glue to the back of the card. Cut out a smaller oval in the centre and snip the excess fabric to form tabs, then glue them to the back of the cardboard.
6. Repeat with the similar piece. Then cover the other two pieces of medium-weight cardboard with the remaining smaller pieces of fabric.
7. Place one plain piece behind one window piece, both with the fabric side up. Oversew neatly together along the top and bottom, and the *left-hand* side only, taking only one or

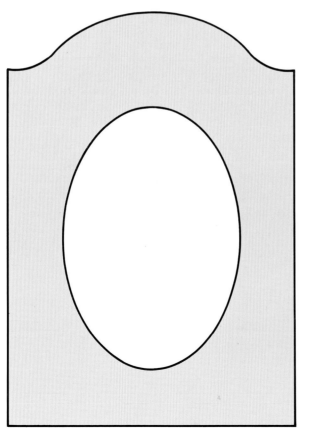

Trace this pattern

two threads of fabric along the edges of the pieces. Repeat with the other two covered pieces, but this time over-sew the right-hand edges together.

8. Place the two pieces together, sandwiched between the two stiff pieces of cardboard. Measure the thickness – adding one-tenth of the total measurement, and note the measurement.

9. Glue the two stiff pieces of card side-by-side to the wrong side of the large piece of fabric, the surplus fabric overlapping equally all round

– and *leaving a space between* equal to the measurement you noted.

10. Mitre and clip into the surplus fabric all round, fold the tabs over and glue to the cardboard.

11. Glue the narrow strip of fabric over the centre gap, overlapping the cardboard on each side.

12. Glue the two frame pieces inside the stiff cover, matching the outer edges carefully, with the stitched sides in the centre.

13. Glue russian braid neatly all round the outer edge.

The camera was one of the most fascinating wonders of the nineteenth century – and the Victorians exploited its potential to the full. Choose a firmly-woven cotton-blend fabric for this professional-looking frame, and you'll find it's deceptively easy to make.

*L*AVENDER SACHETS

*Tiny lavender sachets – or pot pourrie if you
prefer – are a timeless token of affection for
someone you are fond of.*

Materials

WARDROBE SACHET

7in (18cm) of printed sheer ribbon,
2¼in (56mm) wide
4¾in (12cm) of lace edging, ⅝in
(15mm) wide
Dried lavender (or fine pot-pourri)
Matching threads
6in (15cm) of ribbon, ³⁄₈in (9mm)
wide
8in (20cm) of satin ribbon, ¹⁄₁₆in
(1.5mm) wide, to hang

Order of work

1. Fold the sheer ribbon across the width, and oversew the sides together, very close to the edge; leave the raw edges open at the top.
2. Sew lace around the top so that it overlaps the raw edge.
3. Three-quarters fill the sachet with lavender, then gather straight across the bag 1in (2.5cm) below the top edge of the lace. Draw up tightly, binding the thread twice round the neck of the sachet before securing it.

4. Trim the sachet with a mock bow 3½in (9cm) wide. (Refer to page 17 for making mock bows.) If you prefer, trim with ribbon roses. (Refer to page 19 for ribbon roses.)
5. Fold the narrow ribbon in half and knot the ends to form a loop, then sew behind the gathered neck.

Materials

DRAWER SACHET

6¾in (17cm) of printed, sheer ribbon,
2¼in (56mm) wide
Dried lavender (or fine pot-pourri)
12in (30cm) of lace edging, ⅜in
(9mm) wide
10½in (26cm) of ribbon, ¼in (6mm)
wide ribbon
Matching threads
Tracing pattern paper
2in (5cm) of green ribbon, 1in
(2.5cm) wide
Fusible tape

Order of work

1. Referring to the diagram (Fig 1), fold the sheer ribbon at B–F so that E meets G and A–B meets C, then oversew E–F–G together, close to the edge. Fold along C–G, taking G–H over F–E, so that H meets F. Oversew together. (This is the back of the sachet.)
2. At the top, oversew B–A to D–C, leaving B–C free for the front of the sachet. Top-stitch along the folds B–F and C–G.

Trace this pattern

Measure and mark the ribbon as indicated.

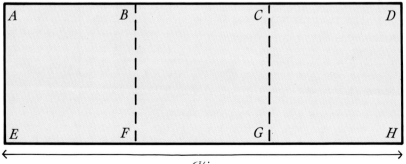

6¾in

3. Fill the sachet with lavender and oversew the top edges together.

4. Sew lace all round the front edge, gathering it to extra fullness at the corners.

5. Trim the sachet with a ribbon rose, made from a 6in (15cm) piece of ¼in (6mm)-wide ribbon, and a mock bow 3½in (8cm) wide made from a 4¼in (11cm) piece of the same ribbon. (Refer to page 17 for making mock bows, and page 19 for ribbon roses.)

ROSE LEAVES. Trace the leaf pattern. Cut out. Bond two pieces of 1in (2.5cm)-wide green ribbon together with fusible tape. Place the paper pattern lengthways on the ribbon and cut out with sharp scissors.

6. Sew on the rose leaf and rose.

Sheer ribbons are the secret of these quick-to-make lavender sachets. The soft floral designs appear hazy and subtle – while the lavender inside is clearly visible.

$\mathscr{P}$ATCHWORK
SEWING SET

A drawstring bag containing all her sewing
accessories would have appealed to a Victorian
mama as both practical and pretty.

Materials

Tracing pattern paper
Medium-weight cardboard
Medium-weight printed cotton as
  follows:
Fabric A 16 x 12in (40 x 30cm)
Fabric B 16 x 8in (40 x 20cm)
Fabric C 8 x 10in (20 x 25cm)
Fabric D 8 x 10in (20 x 25cm)
Matching sewing threads
Fusible interfacing
20in (50cm) of seam binding
1yd (90cm) of heavy lace edging,
  ⅝in (15mm) wide
Dry stick adhesive
1yd (90cm) of double-face satin
  ribbon, ⅛in (3mm) wide
Washable polyester toy filling
White felt 6½ x 4¾in (16 x 12cm)
Heavyweight interfacing 6 x 4in
  (15 x 10cm) wide
14in (35cm) of braid, ¼ – ⅜in
  (6–9mm) wide
Small press fastener
6in (15cm) of double-face satin
  ribbon, ⅛in (3mm) wide
Clear adhesive

Order of work

NEEDLEWORK BAG

1. Trace hexagons a and b *very accurately* onto cardboard and cut round line b: then cut away the centre (line a) to make a window template. Place the card template on the wrong side of the fabric and pencil round both the outer and inner edges. Then cut out the fabric hexagons on the outer line.

2. Cut one patch in fabric A, and six each in fabrics B, C and D.

3. To make up the patches, fold the cut edges to the wrong side along the inner marked line, turning the corners very neatly and basting to hold them in place.

4. Make up the hexagon patchwork as follows: place patches together, right sides facing. Oversew the six fabric D patches around the fabric A hexagon. Use very tiny stitches, taking only a thread of fabric on each side of the seam. Then sew the fabric B and C patches, alternating, around the outside of the rosette of patches. Press very thoroughly.

5. Remove all the basting threads *except* those around the outer edge. Cut a piece of fusible interfacing to the same shape as the patch, but slightly smaller, and iron it onto the back of the hexagon.

6. Cut the bag in fabric A 15 x 9in (38 x 23cm). Matching the centre of the hexagon to the centre of the fabric, iron the hexagon onto the right side. Then slip-stitch all round the outer edge. Remove the basting threads.

7. Right sides facing, fold the bag in half and stitch the two short edges together. The bag now measures 7½ x 9in (19 x 23cm).

8. Turn the top 1in (2.5cm) over to

In patchwork, it is important to use a firmly-woven cotton-blend fabric to ensure a successful result.

the wrong side and baste. Stitch seam binding over the raw edge to form a channel. Unpick a few stitches in the side seams just over the channel.

9. Turn the bag to the right side and stitch lace around the top edge.

10. Cut the double-face ribbon in half and thread each piece through the channel to form drawstrings. Knot the ends and adjust the ribbons so that the knots are inside the channel, out of sight. Bringing the loops through the seam at each side, work one or two stitches on the open, unpicked seams so that the seams hold.

PIN-CUSHION

11. Trace and make card templates for the hexagon, following lines b and c. Trace the square template on the inner and outer lines. Cut two hexagons in fabric D, and three squares each in fabrics B and C.

12. Cut the *inner hexagon* (line b) once in cardboard, and the *inner square* six times in cardboard.

13. Using dry stick adhesive, glue the card hexagon to the wrong side of one fabric patch, for the base of the pin-cushion. Then turn the excess fabric over neatly and glue it to the back of the cardboard. Make up the six squares in the same way.

14. Cover the second cardboard hexagon in the same way for the top of the pin-cushion.

15. Oversew the side edges of the squares together, to form a circle, right sides outside. Oversew the top hexagon to the top edge of the circle. Oversew three sides of the base hexagon to the bottom of the circle. Stuff the pin-cushion, then continue sewing the base into place, adding more stuffing before completing the seam. Sew lace around the top edge.

Trace the patterns for the hexagon and square templates. Trace the scissors case pattern.

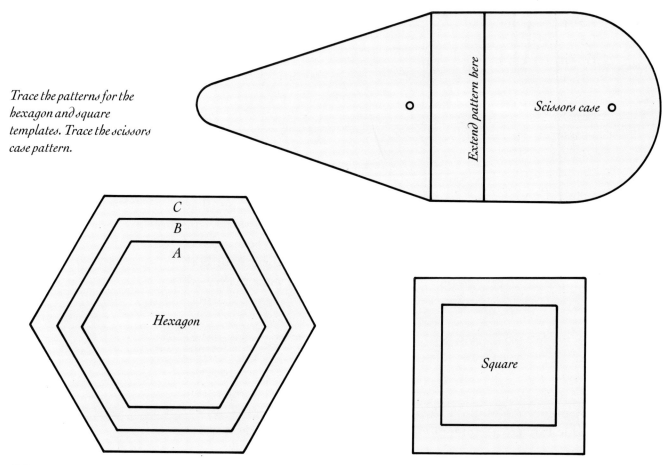

Extend pattern here

Scissors case

C
B
A

Hexagon

Square

Adjust the size of the scissors case as instructed to fit your own scissors. Then buy pins, needles, a thimble and a skein of mixed sewing threads to complete a set that every needlewoman would be delighted to receive.

NEEDLE BOOK

16. Cut two pieces of cardboard 3 x 2¼in (7.5 x 6cm). Cut two pieces of fabric B ⅝in (15mm) larger all round. Cut two pieces slightly smaller than the cardboard.

17. Using dry stick adhesive, glue the pieces of cardboard to the wrong side of the larger pieces of fabric. Mitre the corners neatly and turn the surplus fabric on the edges over and glue to the back of the cardboard. Glue the smaller pieces of fabric neatly over the back.

18. Cut two pieces of felt 2¾ x 4in (7 x 10cm). Stitch them together down the centre, then fold to form 'pages'.

19. Sandwich the felt pages between the pieces of card, then oversew together down one long edge, catching in the folded felt.

20. Cut a strip of fabric 3 x 1in (7.5 x 2.5cm) and glue it over the spine of the needle book.

21. Glue lace over the raw edge of the spine to finish the book.

SCISSORS CASE

22. Trace the pattern and cut it out. Check that your scissors will fit the case when the flap is folded down and the 'o's meet. If your scissors are too long, extend the pattern at the point indicated.

23. Cut the whole pattern once in heavyweight interfacing, and then cut the front section only. Iron fusible interfacing onto both sides of both pieces. Bond fabric A to both sides of the larger piece of interfacing. Bond fabric C to both sides of the front section.

24. Oversew the two pieces together. Glue braid all round the outside edge. Sew on the press fastener at the points marked 'o' on the pattern. Make a ribbon rose (refer to page 19) and glue it over the fastener on the outside flap.

THE VICTORIAN CHRISTMAS SAMPLER

*Every little girl's education consisted of
reading, writing, arithemetic – and learning to
sew. Stitching a sampler taught her all four.*

Samplers go back to the sixteenth century, when they were originally 'needlework notes' worked on a piece of linen, and kept in one's work-box as a reminder of stitches and patterns that might prove useful in the future. But by the time little Victorian girls were stitching their samplers, intriguing trees, animals, birds and tiny figures often illustrated the life of the stitcher.

Antique samplers are much sought after today, and if they are in good condition, can command high prices. Unfortunately, many have been damaged by damp, or have faded badly due to many years exposure to the light.

The collection of motifs in this sampler are all connected with Christmas – and they can be used in two ways. You can design your own Christmas sampler, picking out those elements that attract you most, either reproducing the complete alphabets, or taking the letters and numerals you need to spell out names or initials, and dates. Or you can select individual motifs to make greeting cards, or to frame as miniature pictures for a nursery, to decorate table linen or to personalize gifts.

The sample is worked on cream Aida fabric with sixteen blocks of threads to 1in (2.5cm), using two strands of stranded embroidery cotton for the cross stitch, and one strand for the backstitch outlines. The gold and silver embroidery is worked with three strands of silver or gold thread. Match thread colours to the pictured sampler.

THE ALPHABETS AND NUMBERS. Use these to make up a Christmas message or a name. The single diagonal stitches in the decorative motif on the capital letters are worked in gold or silver. Dot the 'i' and 'j' in the lower case alphabet with French knots.

THE FRONT DOOR. Make long stitches across the pale blue fanlight to divide it into panes, couching them down with a single strand. Outline the door frame and tubs with dark brown, and the inner panels with mid-brown.

THE SNOWMAN. Outline the snow with dark blue. Use four strands of black thread together and work straight stitches over two blocks for the hat brim.

SANTA CLAUS. Outline the sack and presents, the hands and fur trimming with black, and also backstitch the inner sides of sleeves. Use two strands of black for the eyes.

PUDDING. Outline the top and plate with mid-brown.

CHRISTMAS ROSE. Outline the deep cream petals with soft brown.

SILVER BELLS. Outline these with dark grey.

ROBIN. Use two strands and work in straight stitches for the beak and leg, but use only one strand for the feet.

STOCKINGS. Outline these with black or a dark, toning colour.

CANDLESTICK. Outline the stand with a darker shade, and the candleglow with orange. Use a single strand of black for the wicks.

LANTERN. Shade outwards from bright yellow to deep orange, then divide the panes with a single strand of black. Use a single strand of dark green for the sprigs of fir.

CRACKERS. Outline with the darkest shade or with a contrasting colour.

GLASS BAUBLES. Work the sprigs of fir with a single strand of dark green.

SKATING GIRL. Outline the bonnet, cape, skirt, petticoat and muff with

darker shades of the main colour. Use two strands of black and work long straight stitches for the skates.

SKATING BOY. Outline the face and hand, hat (but not pompon), scarf, tunic, sleeve, trousers and boots with dark shades of the main colour. Make

a French knot for the eye. Use two strands of black and work long, straight stitches for the skates.

THE BORDER. Work a row of cross stitches then the heart and star motif. The lacy outer edging is worked with a single strand of cotton.

Stitch the individual motifs separately for Christmas cards, small pictures or to decorate linen. Or use the chart to design your own complete sampler, and make a wonderful family heirloom.

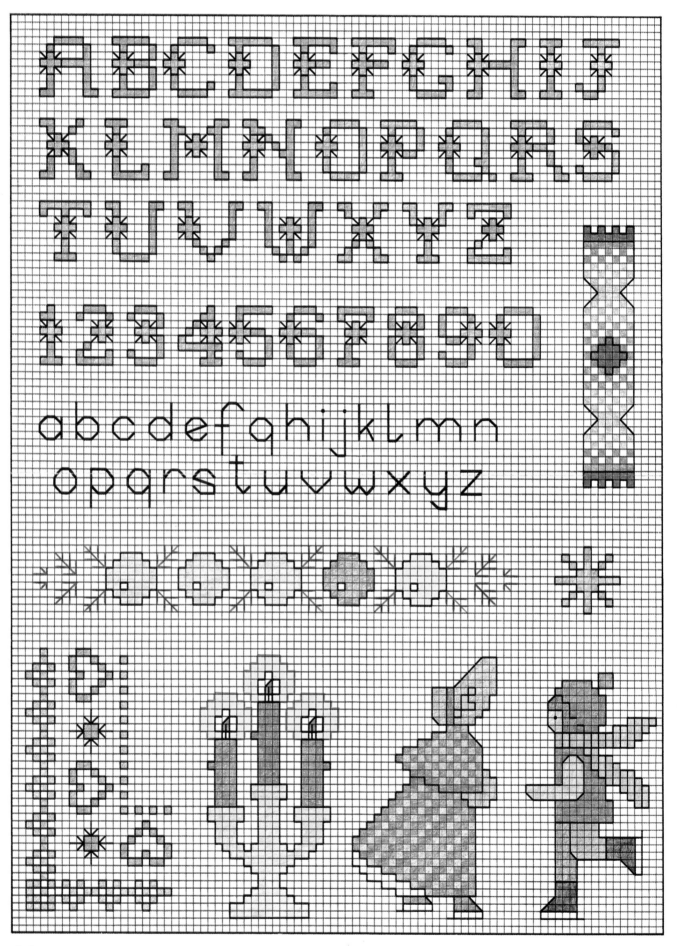

THE FINISHING TOUCH OF NOSTALGIA

Although the Victorians did not wrap their gifts in Christmas papers and ribbons, here are some ideas for wrappings almost too pretty to take off!

Helichrysum flowers, set against sprigs of blossom and backed with a doily, make unusually pretty greeting cards.

Children among the carol-singers might have been lucky enough to receive a sugar mouse off the tree, as well as the customary mince pie. Little packets of sweet candies and candied fruits would have been colourfully wrapped to decorate the tree, but it was only in the latter part of the century – with the arrival of Santa Claus – that the Victorians began to exchange Christmas presents. And even then, there is little evidence to show that they gift-wrapped them as we do today; plain brown or white paper was used, and sealing wax instead of sticky tape.

But had they done so, there's no doubt that they would have done it with artistry and enthusiasm. Since the Victorians loved to adorn anything with ribbons and flowers and beautiful bows – perhaps it isn't too much to imagine how they *might* have done it! All the packages here are wrapped in shimmering foil which folds smoothly and easily: some are paper-backed, making them specially good for all kinds of craftwork. Once the gift is wrapped, you are free to go over the nostalgic top to create the Victoriana effect!

Floral gift cards

Use small, blank greetings cards to make very special gift tags. Little 'cocktail' doilies evoke a suitably Victorian background for an arrangement of dried flowers and foliage, securely glued into position. Set broom, sea lavender and strawflowers against coloured foil doilies. A dainty white doily makes a romantic setting for a pink strawflower surrounded by broom. (Broom was traditionally included in a Victorian bride's bouquet – and also strewn before her on the bridal path as she went to church.)

Tiny boxes, trimmed with twisted gift ribbon and sprigs of dried flowers make simple gifts look very special.

Ribbons and Roses boxes

An extra-wide floral-print sheer ribbon surrounds the silver-wrapped parcel, centred with a toning, narrower, plain sheer ribbon. This plain ribbon, 1in (2.5cm) wide, is used to make the giant cabbage rose that nestles amid the double bow on top. (Refer to page 19 to make the rose, and use up to 2yd (2m) of ribbon. Directions for the mock bows are on page 17.)

Paper ribbon ties the golden parcel, the giant bow centred with a gold satin rose made from 1yd (1m) of 1in (2.5cm)-wide ribbon, and sprigs of broom.

Miniature parcels

Little boxes are perfect for small but precious trinkets – or they could hold a single, rich chocolate truffle,

or a few sugared almonds. To make a square box, draw a square on a thin piece of cardboard – a 1½in (4cm) square is a good size. Then draw squares from each of the four sides, plus one more square on one of the new squares. This is for the lid. Cut out the shape and then score along the lines, using the back of a crafts knife.

Fold up the box and tape the sides, leaving the lid open. Fill with sweets, candies or a small gift wrapped in tissue. Tape the lid into place. Wrap the little box in foil giftwrap and tie with very narrow ribbon. Slip tiny pieces of dried foliage under the ribbon (bind the stalks with stem tape if necessary). Glue the flowers in place. If the boxes are to be hung on the tree, thread very fine gold thread through the narrow ribbon and knot the ends to make a small loop.

PRESENTS TO COOK

*The Victorians loved to cook delicious
presents — luscious preserved fruits,
sweets, candies and tasty gingerbread men.*

CHOCOLATE PRALINES

— ❋ —

Ingredients

1lb (500g/scant 2½ cups) Caster
(superfine) Sugar

Lemon juice

12oz (375g/scant 2½ cups) whole
Hazelnuts, skinned

4oz (125g/1 cup) whole blanched Almonds

Flavourless cooking Oil for baking sheet

3½oz (100g/3½ squares) good-quality
plain (dark) Chocolate, melted

*Nougat and pralines are the
perfect sweetmeats to serve
after a festive meal.*

Method

1. Melt the sugar with a few drops of lemon juice, then mix in the nuts (which have been warmed in the oven). Heat until a rich golden brown. Immediately pour the mixture onto a well-oiled baking tray.
2. Leave until cold and set.
3. Break the praline and process to a fine paste then gradually add melted chocolate, keeping a little back.
4. Mould the mixture into balls and dip in the remaining melted chocolate. Leave to harden.

Makes 2¼ lb (1.2kg)

NOUGAT

— ❋ —

Ingredients

1¼ lb (625g/scant 3 cups) Caster
(superfine) Sugar

16 fl oz (500ml/2 cups) Water

6oz (175g/½ cup) clear Honey

6oz (175g/½ cup) liquid Glucose

3oz (75g/scant ⅓ cup) Egg whites

3oz (75g/generous ½ cup) Glacé Cherries
and canned fruit, mixed

2oz (50g/scant ½ cup) Pistachio nuts

3oz (75g/generous ½ cup) whole
Hazelnuts, toasted

3½oz (100g/⅔ cup) whole blanched
Almonds, toasted

Rice paper

Method

1. Boil the sugar and water to 107°C (225°F). Add the honey and glucose and cook to 135°C (225°F).
2. Whisk the egg whites until stiff and gradually whisk in the hot liquid. Continue to beat until the mixture becomes a firm consistency (it takes a while). Mix in the rest of the ingredients.
3. Line a tin with rice paper. Spoon in the mixture and press down well. Leave overnight to set.
4. Cut the nougat into 1in (2.5cm) squares.
5. The squares can be dipped in melted chocolate, if desired.

Makes 3¼lb (1.8kg)

SUGAR MICE
— ❋ —
Ingredients

1½lb (750g/3½ cups) Caster (superfine) Sugar
16fl oz (500ml/2 cups) Water
Pinch of Cream of Tartar
1tsp (5ml) Rosewater
Edible liquid Red Food Colouring
Vanilla essence (extract)

Method

1. Melt the sugar in the water, add the cream of tartar and boil to a soft ball stage 110°C (225°F). Pour onto a cold work surface and leave until lukewarm. Using a metal scraper (or palette knife) vigorously work the fondant by scraping it from the surface and turning the edges to the middle, until it becomes thick.
2. Knead with moistened hands until perfectly smooth.
3. Knead the rosewater into half the fondant and colour with food

colouring. Be very, very sparing as only a tiny drop is needed to achieve the delicate shade required. Flavour the other half with a few drops of vanilla essence (extract).
4. Allow to rest for a short time.
5. Divide both fondants into 6–8 pieces.
6. Make two tiny balls the size of peas from each piece then roll the remainder into teardrop shapes, flattening them slightly.
7. Flatten the tiny balls and pinch the edges and press them onto the mice bodies for ears. Make eyes with a cocktail stick or toothpick. Leave the mice in a cool dry place to harden.
8. When partially dry, poke in the knotted end of a piece of string for the tail.

Makes 12–16 sugar mice
Note: 2lb (1kg) of ready-made fondant can be substituted in this recipe.

Children will enjoy making sugar mice. Ready-made fondant can be bought to make the task quick and easy, though making your own always makes the mice extra-special.

Preserved cherries and pears make a lovely Christmas gift.

PRESERVED CHERRIES

Ingredients

3lb (1.5kg) sweet Cherries

1½lb (750g/3½ cups) Caster (superfine) Sugar

¾pint (450ml/scant 2 cups) Water

Method

1. Wash and dry the cherries thoroughly. Prick each one with a pin to prevent them from bursting during cooking.
2. Boil the sugar and water to a syrup, add the cherries and simmer gently for 10 minutes.
3. Drain the fruit with a slotted spoon and pack them into clean, sterilized jars.
4. Pour over the hot syrup and seal the jars in the usual way.

Makes 4lb (2kg)

PICKLED PEARS

Ingredients

2lb (1kg) hard Pears

Juice of 1 Lemon

2 Cinnamon sticks

8 Allspice berries

4 whole Cloves

2 dried Chillies

1oz (25g) fresh root Ginger, peeled and sliced

1 pint (600ml/2½cups) White Wine Vinegar

1¾lb (875g/1½cups) Caster (superfine) Sugar

Method

1. Peel, quarter and core the pears. Place them in a saucepan of water with the lemon juice. Bring to the boil and simmer gently for about one hour, or until the fruit is just tender.
2. Meanwhile, place the remaining ingredients in a large pan and heat gently, stirring until the sugar has melted.
3. Bring to the boil and simmer for five minutes. Remove from the heat.
4. Carefully lift the pears from the water and place in the spiced vinegar syrup.
5. Simmer for 15–20 minutes or until the pears look translucent and are very tender.
6. Drain the pears on kitchen paper and then pack into clean, preheated jars. Boil the syrup for about five minutes to thicken, then pour over the pears to cover them.
7. Cover and seal in the usual way and store in a cool dry place.

Makes 2lb (1kg)

GINGERBREAD MEN
— ❄ —
Ingredients

8oz (250g/1⅔ cups) plain (all-purpose)
    Flour
2 tsp (10ml) Baking Powder
1–2 tsps (5–10ml) ground Ginger
3oz (75g/⅓ cup) Butter
2oz (50g/generous ⅓ cup) Caster
    (superfine) Sugar
2 tblsp (30ml) Treacle (molasses)
1–2 tblsp (15–30ml) Milk

Method

1. Sift the flour with the baking powder and ground ginger. Rub in the butter until the mixture resembles fine breadcrumbs.
2. Mix in the sugar, warmed treacle (molasses) and milk. Knead until smooth and roll out to ¼in (6mm) thick. Cut out men with a cutter. Transfer to a greased baking sheet.
3. Leave to rest in a refrigerator for 20–30 minutes. Bake in a pre-heated oven 190°C (375°F/Gas 5) for 10–12 minutes. Transfer to a cooling rack.

Makes: about 8

BRANDY SNAPS
— ❄ —
Ingredients

2oz (50g/¼ cup) Butter, softened
4oz (125g/scant ⅔ cup) Caster
    (superfine) Sugar
2oz (50g/¼ cup) Golden Syrup (corn
    syrup)
2oz (50g/⅓ cup) plain (all-purpose)
    Flour
¼ tsp ground Ginger
Cooking Oil for baking sheet

Method

1. Cream the butter and sugar together until light and fluffy. Beat in the syrup then fold in the flour and ginger.
2. Mould the mixture into walnut-sized pieces and press onto a well-oiled baking sheet. Do only two or three at a time and keep them well spaced.
3. Bake at 160°C (325°F/Gas 3) for 5–8 minutes until golden.
4. When ready, remove the snaps from the oven, cool very slightly. Then lift the snaps carefully with a knife blade and mould over a cornet mould or round the handle of an oiled wooden spoon.
5. Leave to cool before removing from the mould or spoon. (This takes only a minute or so.)

Makes: about 8

Brandy snaps and gingerbread men are as popular today as they were with the Victorians. The features on the gingerbread men can be indicated with dried fruit or dabs of glacé icing.

CHAPTER EIGHT

God rest ye merry gentlemen ...

CAROLS, MINCE PIES AND PUNCH

ALL THE POPULAR CHRISTMAS CAROLS
REMINDED THE VICTORIANS THAT NOW WAS
THE TIME TO OPEN WIDE THE DOOR AND
OFFER HOSPITALITY. A BOWL OF PUNCH
PROVIDED A WARM WELCOME, WITH ITS
WONDERFUL AROMA OF SPICED WINE AND
CITRUS FRUITS, AND EVERY FAMILY HAD ITS
OWN CLOSELY GUARDED RECIPE. THE FRUITY
MINCEMEAT IN THE MINCE PIES COULD BE
LACED WITH SPIRIT TOO: AND IT WAS
ESSENTIAL TO EAT ONE EVERY DAY UNTIL
TWELFTH NIGHT, TO ENSURE GOOD FORTUNE
IN THE COMING YEAR.

Despite its new image, the Victorian 'family' Christmas still needed a visit from the waits to set the mood. Each night, in the weeks before Christmas, bands of strolling musicians toured the towns and villages, just as the mummers had done years before, singing carols to the householders. Their instruments might include fiddles, serpents (a kind of woodwind instrument), clarinets and handbells. After performing, they were generally given money or a drink. However, the entertainment became so raucous that eventually it became a public nuisance, and towards the end of the century the waits were banned by law.

The waits were replaced by choristers from the parish church, who carried only a lantern and usually sang their carols unaccompanied. They were always invited in for a warm drink and a mince pie – and sometimes a donation towards a feast on Twelfth Night.

Like so many other Christmas customs, the singing of carols is pagan in origin, and was only adopted later by the Christian church. The French were the first to sing carols: they began to take on a religious nature in the fourteenth century, and were popular because the words and music were simple and unsophisticated. Carols were suppressed in the mid-seventeenth century by the Puritans, and did not enjoy a real come-back until they were revived by the Victorians two hundred years later.

The mince pies that the Victorians handed around were made just as they are now. But the mince pie is steeped in history. Originally known as Christmas pies, they were savoury: in one old recipe, the mixture inside the pastry crust includes geese, turkeys, ducks, rabbits, curlews, blackbirds, pigeons, partridges, snipe and woodcock. The pies were often made in an oval shape, to represent the manger in which the Christ child was laid, and sometimes they even contained a little pastry baby. But this custom died out when the Puritans decided that the eating of mince pies – especially by clergymen – was a disgrace, and the making of them became illegal. Fortunately, the mince pie was restored with the monarchy in 1660.

'A merry Christmas, Bob!' said Scrooge, with an earnestness that could not be mistaken, as he clapped him on the back. 'A merrier Christmas, Bob, my good fellow, than I have given you for many a year! I'll raise your salary, and endeavour to assist your struggling family, and we will discuss your affairs this very afternoon, over a Christmas bowl of smoking bishop, Bob!'

From *A Christmas Carol* by Charles Dickens

Kate Greenaway's illustration depicts small children playing at being strolling musicians, known as 'waits'. These toured the towns and villages before Christmas, collecting money.

Over the centuries, the mixture gradually changed to the sweet one that is made in Britain today, consisting of dried fruit, candied peel, chopped almonds, apples and suet and, possibly, some alcohol. Occasionally, especially in America, the mixture still included meat – usually chopped lean beef.

It was important to eat a mince pie on each of the Twelve Days of Christmas – each in a different house – as this would ensure twelve happy months in the coming year. However, if you hadn't the willpower to resist scoffing all twelve before Twelfth Night, you could still be pretty certain of good times ahead.

Apart from mince pies, the hospitable Victorians had plenty of other temptations to hand round – roasted chestnuts, fresh and candied fruits, preserved figs, marzipan sweetmeats, gingerbread and nuts.

The warming drink that the carol-singers were offered might well have been punch. This is another tradition that has its origins in the distant past, when a wassail bowl containing 'lambswool' – a mixture of hot ale with eggs, spices, sugar, cream, roasted apples and tiny bits of toast – would have been handed around so that everyone could drink from it in turn.

By the time this convivial beverage reached the Victorians, it was a mixture of wine, spirits, citrus fruit, cloves and spices, sugar and hot water. Each family had its own closely guarded recipe, which was expertly prepared in a large, deep, china bowl, and ladled out by the host. The aromatic mixture of oranges, lemons, spiced wine and spirits must have had a wonderfully warming effect on a cold night.

Claret cup was another popular Victorian tipple. Two glasses of dry sherry were poured into a quart container, then a little nutmeg and a few cloves added, together with two tablespoons of sugar, some lemon rind and juice and either mint and cucumber or a sprig of borage. Then a little claret was stirred in and the mixture left to stand for twenty minutes – before removing all the bits and pieces. When the cup was required, two bottles of soda were poured in before filling up with claret.

WELCOMING TREATS

Greet unexpected guests — or see friends
on their way — with a heartwarming drink
and a traditional, spicy mince pie.

BISHOP

Ingredients

2 Lemons

6 Cloves

8 floz (250ml/1 cup) Water

1 bottle of Port

1 Cinnamon stick

1 blade of Mace

6 Allspice berries

3–4 slices of root Ginger

2oz (50g) cubed Sugar

Method

1. Stick one lemon with the cloves and bake in the oven at 190°C (375°F/Gas 5) for 20 minutes.
2. Bring the water and port to the boil with the cinnamon stick, mace, allspice and ginger. Cover and leave for 20 minutes.

3. Return to the boil, add the baked lemon. Cover and leave to stand for a further 5 minutes.
4. Rub the sugar cubes on the rind of the other lemon and place them in the bottom of a bowl. Squeeze the juice from half of the lemon and add to the bowl. Pour in the port. Stir and serve at once.

Serves: 10

CIDER CUP

Ingredients

1 wine glass Brandy

2oz (50g/⅓ cup) Caster (superfine) Sugar

A few thin strips of Cucumber Peel

Juice and pared rind of 1 Lemon

Ice cubes

1¾ pints (1 litre/4½ cups) Cider, chilled

1¾ pints (1 litre/4½ cups) Soda water, chilled

Method

1. Stir the brandy and sugar together in a large punch bowl until the sugar has melted. Stir in the cucumber, lemon rind and juice and ice cubes. Add the chilled cider and soda and serve at once.

Serves: 8–10

Bishop punch can be gently re-heated before serving in warmed glasses.

MINCE PIES
— ❋ —
Ingredients

8oz (250g/1⅔ cups) plain (all-purpose)
*   Flour*
4oz (125g/½ cup) Butter
1 tblsp (15ml) Caster (superfine) Sugar
2 Egg yolks
12–16oz (375–500g/2–2½ cups) Spicy
*   Mincemeat*
A little Milk
Caster (superfine) Sugar for dredging

Method

1. Rub the butter lightly into the flour. Add the sugar and egg yolks and a little cold water.
2. Mix to a stiff dough.
3. Chill, wrapped in plastic film, until ready to use.
4. Roll out the pastry to ¼in (6mm) thick. Using 3in (7.5cm) pastry cutters, cut out about twenty rounds. Cut another twenty, slightly smaller, rounds for the lids.
5. Press the larger rounds into patty tins (muffin pans) and spoon in the mincemeat. Brush water around the edges and seal on the smaller rounds.

6. Brush lightly with a little milk. Make a small hole with a skewer and bake at 200°C (400°F/Gas 6) for 25-30 minutes. Dredge the tops with caster (superfine) sugar. Serve hot or cold.

Makes about 20

SPICY MINCEMEAT
— ❋ —
Ingredients

8oz (250g) Cooking Apples, peeled, cored
*   and chopped*
2oz (50g/⅓ cup) dried Figs, chopped
4oz (125g/¾ cup) Muscatel Raisins
4oz (125g/⅔ cup) Sultanas (golden
*   raisins)*
4oz (125g/¾ cup) Currants
2oz (50g/⅓ cup) mixed Candied Peel,
*   chopped*
2oz (50g/⅓ cup) whole blanched Almonds,
*   chopped*
4oz (125g/¾ cup) soft dark brown Sugar
Grated rind and juice of half a Lemon
½ tsp (2.5ml) of ground Cinnamon
Large pinch of ground Nutmeg
½ tsp (2.5ml) of ground Ginger
Large pinch of ground Cloves
2oz (50g) Suet (optional)
2floz (60ml/¼ cup) of Brandy

Method

1. Put the apples, dried fruit and candied peel through a mincer or food processor. Add the other ingredients and mix well.
2. Spoon into jars and press down well to exclude air. Seal.
3. Store in a cool, dry place for one month for the flavours to develop.

Makes approximately 2lb/1kg

Whisky can be substituted for brandy in the mincemeat recipe – or drip it through the hole of the piecrust after cooking.

One recipe for punch called for the rind of three lemons and the juice of ten; the rind of two Seville oranges and the juice of four. The rind was cut into very thin strips.

Six glasses of melted calves-foot jelly were placed in a hot jug and four pints of boiling water stirred in. While it was left to cool a little, a pint of French brandy, a pint of white wine and a glassful of crushed sugar were placed in the punch-bowl, together with Jamaica rum or orange cordial. Then the cooled liquid was poured over.

$\mathscr{I}$NDEX

ACKNOWLEDGEMENTS

My most sincere thanks to both my editors, Eve Harlow and Kate Yeates, for all their help, enthusiasm and encouragement during the preparation of this book. And to Di Lewis for her superbly evocative photography. I would also like to thank the following companies and individuals for their kind interest and great help in providing materials and properties for the projects in the book:

DMC Embroidery Threads for the threads and fabrics used for the cross stitch designs.

Hallmark Cards Ltd for the coloured foil paper and gift-ties. Also for the illustration of the first Christmas card on page 60.
   C. M. Offray & Son Ltd, Ashford, Middlesex for beautiful ribbons.
   The Handicraft Shop, Canterbury, Kent for turned paper balls, cream felt, trimmings and other craft items.
   Artisan, Pinner, Middlesex for patchwork and Christmas fabrics.
   Victorian Bedrooms, Hungerford, Berkshire for the loan of the Victorian brass bed.
   Susan Smith, Potties and Posies, Hungerford, Berkshire for the loan of Victorian reproduction toys.

Picture Credits

The pictures and illustrations on the following pages are reproduced with the permission of:
   Mary Evans Picture Library: endpapers (and p12); p4 (and 71); p25; p26; p35; p42; p44; p45; p60; p68; p70; p85.
   The Bridgeman Art Library: p8; p9; p13; p24; p34; p43; p61; p72; p84; p106; p107.
   Mansell Collection: p3; p15; p27; p61; p69; p71.
   Hallmark Cards Limited: P60.